Coaching and Mentoring

Harvard Business Essentials

The New Manager's Guide and Mentor

The Harvard Business Essentials series is designed to provide comprehensive advice, personal coaching, background information, and guidance on the most relevant topics in business. Drawing on rich content from Harvard Business School Publishing and other sources, these concise guides are carefully crafted to provide a highly practical resource for readers with all levels of experience, and will prove especially valuable for the new manager. To assure quality and accuracy, each volume is closely reviewed by a specialized content adviser from a world-class business school. Whether you are a new manager seeking to expand your skills or a seasoned professional looking to broaden your knowledge base, these solution-oriented books put reliable answers at your fingertips.

Other books in the series:

Finance for Managers
Hiring and Keeping the Best People
Managing Change and Transition
Negotiation
Business Communication
Managing Projects Large and Small
Manager's Toolkit
Crisis Management
Entrepreneur's Toolkit

Coaching and Mentoring

How to Develop Top Talent and
Achieve Stronger Performance

Harvard Business School Press | *Boston, Massachusetts*

Copyright 2004 Harvard Business School Publishing Corporation
All rights reserved
Printed in the United States of America
08 07 06 05   5 4 3

Library of Congress Cataloging-in-Publication Data
Harvard business essentials : coaching and mentoring.
p. cm. — (The Harvard business essentials series)
Includes bibliographical references and index.
ISBN 1-59139-435-X
1. Mentoring in business. I. Title: Coaching and mentoring.
II. Harvard Business School. III. Series.
HF5385.H27 2004
658.3'124—dc22
2004002699

Contents

Coaching and Mentoring

Introduction

Well-managed companies pay close attention to the development of their human resources. They handle development as part of a larger system of performance management that includes performance appraisal, formal training, and rewards. But these formal programs are just the most obvious means of making the most of human assets. Less obvious but equally important are the day-to-day manager-employee (and executive-manager) interactions that fortify skills, expand knowledge, and inculcate desirable workplace values. This book focuses on two of those interactions: coaching and mentoring.

Coaching is an activity through which managers work with subordinates to foster skill development, impart knowledge, and inculcate values and behaviors that will help them achieve organizational goals and prepare them for more challenging assignments. Coaching is often the byproduct of performance appraisal. Most of the time, however, it takes place in the course of everyday business, whenever a perceptive manager sees a way to help subordinates do things better. The importance of coaching has grown as organizational structures have flattened and the necessity for continual learning is recognized.

Mentoring, like coaching, is a means of developing human resources. Mentoring is about guiding others in their personal quests for growth through learning. The mentor acts as a trusted guide, offering advice when asked and opening doors to learning opportunities when possible and appropriate. Unlike coaching, the initiative in mentoring comes from the person seeking greater understanding. That person—the protégé—must take responsibility for his or her own growth and development.

What's Ahead

Chapters 1 through 5 contain information and practical advice that will make you a better coach. Chapter 1 explains the benefits of coaching and how it aims to accomplish one of two things: (1) to solve performance problems or (2) develop employee capabilities. This material will help you identify the people who need coaching, and will introduce you to a four-step process for doing it right.

Preparation is the first step. Everything worth doing is done better with preparation, and coaching is no exception. Have you identified people who would benefit from coaching? If you have, chapter 2 will help you prepare for the task, beginning with observation, followed by listening and asking questions. Once you've developed and tested a theory for what needs fixing, you'll be ready for chapter 3, which explains the next phase of good coaching: direct discussion with the employee. Here you'll learn how to use open-ended and closed questions to obtain the information you need. You will also learn how to be an active listener, and how to move discussion to the causes of the performance problems or deficiencies you mean to remedy through coaching.

Once you understand the person who needs help and the situation itself, you will be ready to begin your coaching sessions, the subject of chapter 4. This is where the wheels meet the road. The chapter explains how to get down to the business of one-on-one coaching, beginning with agreement on goals and moving on to an action plan on which you and the other person can agree. It will show you how best to communicate and to handle feedback, and emphasizes the importance of follow-up on coaching sessions—coaching rarely works if no one follows up.

Following the four steps of coaching will get you started, but they won't make you a great coach. Chapter 5 will take you beyond the fundamentals. Good coaching is often the product of personal qualities and social skills that cannot be taught in any book. Nevertheless, you can learn some things that will make your coaching experiences better; for example, knowing when to coach and, because some problematic situations are better resolved through other means, when not to. In other circumstances, coaching can sometimes be delegated to competent subordinates, saving time for the busy manager. This chapter can help you to identify situations in which delegation makes sense. It will also explain how you can create a climate in which coaching success is more likely. Finally, you will learn a number of do's and don'ts that can make you a better coach.

Chapter 6 is about the growing field of executive coaching. Executive coaching provides a one-on-one customized approach to altering the behavior of senior people, with the goal of improving on-the-job performance. The coach in these instances is generally an outside specialist hired by the CEO or the board of directors. You'd think that people at the executive level would not need coaching, but in fact many executives have bad habits that need correcting. Some executives create ill will and low morale through arrogance—about which they are totally clueless. Others have never learned to delegate or to work with a team of peer executives—both serious weaknesses for anyone in a senior position. Still others do not know how to collaborate with people in other functions; they got to the top tier by aggressively pushing their own interests; now they must do what's best for the entire organization—they need to learn how to subjugate their own interests and how to collaborate with others. Because it is generally cheaper and less disruptive to cure these habits than to replace top people, corporations try to cure these faults through executive coaching. This chapter explains the potential benefits of executive coaching and the two basic approaches taken by today's managers.

Chapter 7 is the first on the subject of mentoring, to which the remaining chapters are devoted. This chapter introduces the subject of mentoring and explains how it differs from coaching, its benefits and challenges, and its role in the development of human assets.

Mentoring is a highly personal experience that requires a good match between mentor and protégé. Chapter 8 addresses the importance of that match, who should be a mentor, and who should play the role of matchmaker. It describes the experience of one company—Bell Canada—in developing a low-cost, Web-based approach to linking people with mentors.

Chapter 9 looks at the mentoring relationship as a two-way street. It identifies the personal characteristics and behaviors of effective mentors and what their protégés must do to make the most of the relationship. Here, mentors will find nine things they must learn to do well, and protégés are encouraged to observe and experiment with different behavioral styles in the workplace.

Since there are generally few women and minorities in the executive ranks, ambitious women and minorities confront a unique challenge in finding suitable mentors. They cannot always find mentors and appropriate role models who are "like them." Chapter 10 deals with this problem and suggests a number of practical steps for reducing it. The chapter also describes research findings on the career tracks of minorities in U.S. corporations, how those tracks have different time-based stages, and what can be done to keep talented minorities from becoming discouraged.

The book's final chapter looks beyond the traditional mentor-protégé pattern to the concepts of peer mentoring and mentoring networks. Peers can deliver some of the same career and psychosocial functions provided by executive mentors—and they are often more accessible. The benefits and drawbacks of peer mentoring are considered. The chapter also describes what happens when ambitious young managers set up networks of peer and traditional mentors to provide the help that peers and individuals often cannot.

The end matter of this book has a number of items you may find helpful. Appendix A is an eight-step primer on how to conduct performance appraisals of your subordinates. Performance appraisal is one of the best ways of spotting coaching opportunities. Appendix B contains two tools that can help you become a better coach: the first is a self-evaluation checklist for coaches, with questions relating to the skills and qualities of effective coaching. Use this for diagnostic purposes and to identify areas of weakness. This checklist can also be downloaded from the Harvard Business Essentials Web site: www. elearning.hbsp.org/businesstools. That site has many other downloadable tools pertaining to finance, hiring and retention, change management, and other subjects covered in the Harvard Business Essentials series. The second tool in appendix B is a checklist you can use in planning a feedback session with people you are either coaching or mentoring.

The appendices are followed by a glossary of coaching and mentoring terms. These terms are italicized the first time they are used in the text; that's your cue that they are contained in the glossary. The end matter also includes a section entitled For Further Reading, which contains a list of articles and books on coaching and mentoring, along with a brief description of their contents. If you want to expand your knowledge of these subjects, the For Further Reading section will get you started.

The material contained in this book draws heavily on the coaching module of Harvard ManageMentor®, an online product of Harvard Business School Publishing, and on articles published in *Harvard Business Review* and other periodicals. It has also benefited greatly from the "coaching" of Susan Alvey, a human resources professional who generously shared her coaching and mentoring experience in a number of organizations over the years, and from the advice and suggestions made by Herminia Ibarra, Professor of Organizational Behavior at INSEAD in Fontainebleau, France.

Like other books in the series, this one is not designed to make you an expert. Nor does it review the academic literature on the subject of coaching and mentoring. It treats, by design, only the essentials of this important subject. It will get you off to a very good start. The balance of what you must learn to be a great coach, mentor, or protégé will come from practice.

1

What Coaching Is All About

Its Place in Management

Key Topics Covered in This Chapter

- *A definition of coaching*

- *The benefits of coaching for managers and their employees*

- *Coaching as a four-step process*

A MANAGER'S JOB is to get results through people and other resources. And with so many industries becoming more reliant on knowledge and service, people and their skills and performance are a top managerial concern. Companies have a huge interest in the capabilities of their employees, which they attempt to develop through formal and on-the-job training and progressive job assignments. They also expect managers and supervisors to develop employee capacity through coaching. What is coaching? *Coaching* is an interactive process through which managers and supervisors aim to solve performance problems or develop employee capabilities. The process relies on collaboration and is based on three components: technical help, personal support, and individual challenge. As described in figure 1-1, these three coaching elements are held together by an emotional bond between the manager/coach and the subordinate/coachee. Because coaching is a person-to-person experience, this sort of bond must be present—and it must be positive if coaching is to succeed.

This chapter explains the benefits of coaching. It will help you identify the people who need it. And it will introduce a four-step process for doing it right.

Benefits

If you are a manager, you're probably wondering why you should become a coach. You already have plenty to do and rarely enough time to do it all. If you are like most managers, your day is consumed

FIGURE 1-1

The Elements of Successful Coaching

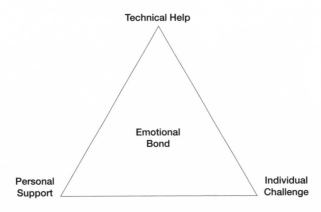

Technical Help

Emotional Bond

Personal Support

Individual Challenge

Source: Susan Alvey, with permission.

by planning, organizing people around projects, dealing with a budget, solving problems, diffusing conflict, sitting through back-to-back meetings, and on and on. So, why coach, given the time and effort involved? The answer is that effective coaching will actually make your job easier and enhance your career by:

- **Overcoming performance problems.** Chances are that you have one or more subordinates who cannot handle the tasks you assign to them. One submits written reports that are chronically disorganized. Another doesn't know how to budget her time. Yet another never contributes anything to weekly staff meetings. Each of these shortcomings makes your job more difficult. Coaching can often solve them.

- **Developing employee skills.** Coaching is a means for developing new skills among employees. Employees with more skills can, in turn, take on some of the routine tasks that currently eat up your time. Your ability to delegate those tasks will give you more time to think, plan, and to motivate others.

- **Increasing productivity.** Impart greater know-how and effectiveness through coaching and people will work smarter. Your unit's performance will improve, and so will your standing in the company.

- **Creating promotable subordinates.** Your own career prospects are determined to some extent by how well you develop the human resources under your command. Are you known as a manager who prepares people for more important roles within the company? Acquire that type of reputation and your star will rise. Also, preparing subordinates to take on large roles will increase your own likelihood of advancement. You will be able to move up because you've developed someone capable of stepping into your shoes.

- **Improving retention.** Are you spending too much of your time interviewing and hiring replacements? Coaching can help by reducing turnover—especially among the people you most want to retain. Why is that? People are more loyal and motivated when their boss takes the time to help them improve their skills. Being a voluntary and collaborative activity, coaching also builds trust between managers and subordinates. And trust translates into greater loyalty.

- **Fostering a positive work culture.** Good coaching produces greater job satisfaction and higher motivation. It may also improve your working relationship with subordinates, making your job as manager much easier.

What's good for you is also good for employees who receive effective coaching. Coaching can help subordinates to rekindle motivation, overcome performance problems, develop their strengths and new skills, and prepare themselves for higher-level jobs.

Identifying Coaching Opportunities

Every situation presents opportunities for coaching. Consider these:

- Jean, a newly appointed supervisor, is overbearing in her dealings with subordinates. Because she lacks supervisory experience, she believes that this approach is the only way to get people to do their jobs.

- Herb is a very accomplished market researcher. His technical skills are superb. But he has few organizational skills and would much rather spend his time at his computer than in meetings with market planners and new product developers. As a result, his valuable findings are not always incorporated into company plans—and his career is going nowhere.

- Claudia has managerial potential. She's a fast learner, works well with other people, and understands the company's goals. You'd like to move her to a higher level, but she isn't quite ready. The one thing that's holding her back is her reluctance to confront difficult and argumentative people. Her upward mobility is checked by this weakness.

- Like other managers, Tim never has enough time to think or plan. "If I could delegate some of my routine chores to Maureen," he tells himself, "I could spend more time on planning." Maureen is a smart and hard worker, but she needs to acquire a few more skills to perform the tasks Tim would like to delegate to her.

Each of these hypothetical situations has something in common: they could probably be improved through coaching. Jean, the "bossy" new supervisor, could be shown that there are other, better ways to get results through people. Herb's genius for market research is underutilized because he doesn't interact with the people who could benefit from his work; he needs to learn some organizational skills. Claudia, too, could be making a larger contribution to her company if she had some pointers and encouragement in confronting difficult people. Finally, Tim, the time-pressed manager, would make his own job easier if he coached Maureen to the point where he could delegate some tasks to her.

Do you observe coaching opportunities like these? Are you letting opportunities to improve performance through coaching slip by? Answer these questions by making a list of all the people you currently deal with who would benefit from effective coaching. Then prioritize the list to identify the three greatest opportunities. Now imagine how much easier your job would be if these people could solve their problems or improve their performance through coaching.

Chances are that every one of your direct reports could benefit from coaching in some way. Your position and experience have given you a mastery of tasks with which others may be struggling. For example, Shirley, the person you recently promoted to supervisor, isn't delegating enough tasks to her subordinates; she's trying to do everything herself. As an experienced manager, you know the importance of delegating and how to do it. You've been honing the art for years, and you could give Shirley some practical tips. Meanwhile, Carlos, one of your other direct reports, is frustrated in his role as leader of the sale support team—a job to which you appointed him several months ago. "Our meetings never seem to produce results," he complains. "People talk and talk and then break for lunch. We never accomplish anything." As an experienced meeting leader, you could help Carlos make his meetings more productive.

Yes, you have plenty of knowledge to share with others—know-how that can improve their performance. But you don't have all the time in the world for sharing it. So target your coaching to situations that most demand it—where you will get the highest return on your commitment of time and effort. These situations generally arise when

- a new subordinate needs direction;

- a direct report is almost ready for new responsibilities and just needs a bit more help; and

- a problem performer could be brought up to an acceptable level of work if he had some guidance

Do you have subordinates like these?

Use Performance Appraisal to Guide Your Coaching

Performance appraisal is often the best instrument for identifying important coaching opportunities. *Performance appraisal* is a formal method used by many companies to assess how well people are doing with respect to their assigned goals. Such an appraisal is generally conducted annually, with follow-ups as needed. Like the physical exam administered by your doctor, this annual checkup gives a manager and the company an opportunity to spot problems before they become chronic. It also helps employees and managers focus on the goals and performance expectations that impact salary, merit pay increases, and result in promotions. Appraisal sessions are both a confirmation and a formalization of the ongoing feedback that should be part of every manager-subordinate relationship.

If a performance appraisal identifies a correctable problem, the manager and subordinate should agree on a plan for eliminating it. Coaching is often part of the plan. The performance appraisal is also used to identify the skills, knowledge, and/or experiences that good employees need to acquire as a condition of moving up a rung on the career ladder. Here again, coaching is often essential to the plan.

Busy managers are not particularly fond of performance appraisals. First, few managers enjoy telling people to their faces that they're not doing their jobs as well as they should. Second, giving performance appraisals to each of many direct reports consumes time, and time is every manager's scarcest asset. Nevertheless, when approached with the right frame of mind and done well, performance appraisal is worth the effort.

Note: If you are unfamiliar with performance appraisals and how to make the most of them, turn to the Appendix A, where you will find an eight-step primer for doing it well.

Intervene Early

Many of your coaching situations will involve personal behaviors or performance problems that you'd rather avoid. One person cannot or will not collaborate with others, or another dominates her team to the point that others are unable to contribute. Yet another is repeatedly late for work. It's always easier to avoid problems like these than to engage with them. If the behavior stems from a personality problem—such as the person who obsessively tries to dominate group activities—few managers will relish the idea of tackling it.

They are managers, after all, not psychologists. Other problems, such as chronic tardiness, may originate in a dysfunctional family situation. Again, few managers want to take on people's personal troubles. Yet correcting problems that reduce performance is part of the manager's job, and doing so is always easier when the intervention is made early. So don't allow bad behavior or performance problems to fester. They won't get better by themselves.

A Four–Step Process

Coaching is generally accomplished through a four-step process of observation, discussion, active coaching, and follow-up. We'll outline these briefly here, and examine them in detail in subsequent chapters.

> **Step 1: Preparation**. The first step in effective coaching is observation. Whether your coaching is done on the spot or at scheduled times and places, you should not do anything until you understand the situation, the person, and the person's current skills. The best way to gain that understanding is through direct observation. Your goal should be to identify the person's strengths and weaknesses and to understand the impact that his behavior is having on coworkers and on his ability to achieve goals.
>
> **Step 2: Discussion**. This step begins with careful preparation. As you prepare, be very clear about the purpose of the discussion, the issues you think are important, and the consequences of not addressing these issues. A prepared coach is a better coach. Once you're prepared, you are ready to engage your subordinate in a dialogue that shares strategies for overcoming performance problems and building skills.
>
> Discussion, in many instances, should lead to a coaching plan on which both parties agree. Bringing performance up to standard within a certain time or risking dismissal is one clear example. A plan assures systematic attention to performance improvement.

Step 3: Active Coaching. Once you understand the person and the situation and you have a plan, coaching sessions should begin. An effective coach offers ideas and advice in such a way that the subordinate can hear them, respond to them, and appreciate their value. Giving and receiving feedback is a critical part of active coaching—and of supervision in general.

Step 4: Follow-Up. Effective coaching includes follow-up that monitors progress. Follow-up helps individuals stay on an improvement trajectory. If they are getting off track, follow-up is your opportunity to get them back on course. Follow-up might include asking what is going well and what is not. "Are you getting stuck?" Follow-up sessions are also opportunities for praising progress and for seeking opportunities for continued coaching and feedback. If the action plan needs modification, the follow-up meeting is the place to do it.

If you're a new manager, or new to coaching, your first efforts may feel uncomfortable and may not be entirely effective. Just remember that you will get better with practice.

Summing Up

- Coaching is an interactive process through which managers and supervisors aim to accomplish one of two things: (1) to solve performance problems, or (2) develop employee capabilities.

- Coaching can help to increase productivity, make subordinates more promotable, and improve retention.

- Performance appraisal often reveals opportunities for coaching.

- Coaching is generally accomplished through a four-step process of observation, discussion, active coaching, and follow-up.

2

Preparing to Coach

Keep Your Eyes, Ears, and Mind Open

Key Topics Covered in This Chapter

- *Beginning with observation, the first step in preparation for coaching*

- *Creating and testing hypotheses based on observation*

- *Listening for signals that help is needed*

- *Meeting the challenge of deeply ingrained problem behavior*

- *Asking employees to prepare for coaching*

LIKE EVERYTHING ELSE, coaching effectiveness is a function of preparation. There will be times, of course, when you must simply jump right in and say, "You appear to be having a problem with this. Can I make a suggestion?" But most of your coaching opportunities will take place at prescheduled times and places. This chapter describes the first step of coaching, preparation, and the many things you can do to set the stage for success.

Begin with Observation

Preparation begins with direct observation, the goal being to understand the situation, the employee, and the employee's current skills and behavior. The insights gained from observing a coachee will enhance your ability to offer informed, relevant, timely advice. These observations can also help you answer the question: Will coaching help this person?

You need to observe the person's behavior both informally (for example, during a meeting) and formally (for example, on joint sales calls). As you observe, learn what the person is not doing well. If you find problems, try to get to the causes. Consider this example:

> While participating in a team meeting, Ralph noted the way Harriet, one of his subordinates, interacted with the group. She had something to say about everything. That was a positive trait, but she repeatedly interrupted others—a negative. Her behavior, in Ralph's estimation, prevented others from expressing their views.

A less observant manager might have said, "Harriet isn't a good team player." But that general statement would not have isolated Harriet's specific problem: knowing when to speak up and when to listen to what others have to say—a problem amenable to coaching.

Avoid Premature Judgments

As you prepare, don't approach the coaching situation with pre-formed judgments. One or two observations may lead to an erroneous conclusion. So continue observing, particularly if you have any doubts about your perceptions, as in the same example.

> *Ralph was annoyed by the way Harriet interrupted and seemed to dominate the meeting he attended. He would have been happier if others had been able to participate more fully. "Does she always behave this way?" he wondered. To find out, he made a point of sitting in on two subsequent meetings attended by Harriet, where he observed the same behavior.*

Observe for Performance Gaps and Skill Deficiencies

A *performance gap* is the difference between a subordinate's current performance and what is required by the job. Here's an example:

> *Scott, a market researcher employed by a regional brokerage firm, is generally effective in his role. However, people who rely on his data and analysis have noted a gap between his performance and job requirements. Specifically, Scott's written reports are poorly organized and often fail to clearly state conclusions.*

A *skill deficiency* is also a gap—between a person's current capabilities and those needed to take on another job—as illustrated in this example:

> *Charlotte knows that she will have a district sales manager position to fill once the current manager retires. Calvin, a successful sales representative in that district, is one of the leading candidates to fill the position. But does he have the skills to do the job? Charlotte has a general impression of Calvin's fitness for the district manager post, but she*

knows that a more empirical evaluation is required. So she begins sys-
tematic observations of Calvin's on-the-job performance: his written
reports, his presentations at sales meetings, his demeanor around col-
leagues and customers, and his approach to solving problems. In each
instance, she is looking for gaps between Calvin's current skills and
performance and what the job of district sales manager requires.

Charlotte began to observe Calvin informally, knowing that a promotion opportunity might arise. But a formal performance appraisal
is a better approach to performance and skills gaps.

Both performance gaps and skill deficiencies can be corrected
through coaching. For instance, in observing Calvin, Charlotte finds
that he is deficient in his ability to make formal presentations to a
group. He is very informal and jocular around customers and his colleagues, and this behavior has probably served him well as a sales representative. But as district sales manager, he will be required to make
serious and detailed presentations to customer committees and his
own company's management. That skill gap must be closed. "I can
show him how to do this," Charlotte tells herself.

Create and Test Your Hypothesis

Observation will eventually lead you to some hypothesis about the
problem or performance gap and its amenability to improvement
through coaching. But your hypothesis may not be valid if your perspective is flawed or limited. To test your hypothesis, ask others what
they think. They may have an entirely different viewpoint. For example, while Ralph may view Harriet's habit of interrupting others
as a deterrent to valuable dialogue, someone else may applaud her
strenuous articulation of her views. So, when appropriate, discuss the
situation with trusted colleagues—in confidence, of course. Add
their observations to your own.

As a final check, Ralph asked another manager, Lena, for a favor.
"Lena," he began, "I notice that you'll be attending my group's plan-
ning meeting this afternoon." She nodded in agreement. "Would you

do something for me?" Ralph went on to ask Lena to observe Harriet's participation in that meeting and let him know her impression. He was careful not to say, "Tell me if she seems to interrupt others." Doing so might have influenced Lena's thinking.

Ralph saw Lena in the coffee room the next day. When no one else was in earshot he asked for her impression of Harriet's participation in the previous day's meeting. "She's smart and very knowledgeable," Lena said. "But she's not a good listener." Ralph asked what made her say that. "Well," Lisa continued, "she interrupts other people when she should be listening to what they have to say."

Listen Carefully

Listening is another element of preparation. Just as you watch for problems, listen for signals that your help and intervention is needed. These signals are not always obvious or direct, as in these examples:

"I can't finish the assignment this month." This person may be saying that he needs your help with time-management problems.

"Perhaps Ed should do this job. He's very good at it." This may be a signal that the person lacks confidence or lacks a particular skill.

"Would you mind if I skipped this week's staff meeting?" Helen asked. "I need to work with Julie that morning." This request may be genuine, but it may be an indication that being at the staff meeting would create a personal conflict Helen wants to avoid.

"Thanks for telling me about the job in the customer service department, but I'm not interested." Why isn't this person interested in applying for a job that you view as a career advance? Is he genuinely not interested or is there another, hidden, reason? Perhaps he feels ill-prepared to take on greater responsibilities.

Don't always accept statements at face value. Instead, look behind them. The subordinates in these examples may be asking for help, but in indirect ways.

If your employees asked for help, would you hear them? People don't always know what kind of help they need or how to ask for it. So take the initiative by asking, "Which part of your job is giving you the most trouble?" Then listen carefully to the response. Approach the same issue from a different angle, if possible, with a different question: "If a new person stepped into your job, what would that person have the most trouble doing well?" Again, listen carefully. Remember that when you are talking you are not learning anything, so spend a minimum amount of time talking and most of the time listening.

Estimate the Probability of Improvement

Once you recognize that an employee has a definable problem, ask yourself "Will coaching improve this situation?" Given the many duties you have as a manager, this is an important question to ask. Coaching a person who *cannot* or *will not* be helped would be a huge waste of your time. The coachee must be motivated to learn and improve.

Coaching cannot improve behavior or performance in all cases. For example, an employee who denies his problem or blames it on others cannot be helped, unless you somehow succeed in convincing him of his error. The same is generally true when a problem behavior is deeply ingrained—to the point of being a habit. Here are some examples of deeply ingrained problem behaviors that are difficult to change through coaching:

- The person who is so competitive that he must always best his peers

- The manager who must always act as the "boss," even when he is a member of a team with an assigned leader

- A manager who insists on solving every problem instead of allowing her subordinates to do so

- An employee who is so lacking in self-confidence that he always defers to others

Writing in *Harvard Business Review*, business psychologists James Waldroop and Timothy Butler framed the likelihood of behavior changes in terms of two factors: (1) the frequency of the troublesome behavior and (2) the depth to which the behavior is entrenched in an employee's persona. Figure 2-1 is an adaptation of their assessment framework. Here, individuals who frequently display bad behaviors *and* who do so as an expression of their inner character are unlikely to respond favorably to coaching. A supervisor who habitually approaches subordinates in an arrogant manner is just one example of an ingrained behavior. In contrast, people whose bad behavior is infrequent and linked to a particular situation are more likely to benefit from coaching. Once you've sized up an employee with this framework, you'll be better able to determine if coaching is the answer.

FIGURE 2-1

Is Coaching the Answer? Assessing the Likelihood of Change

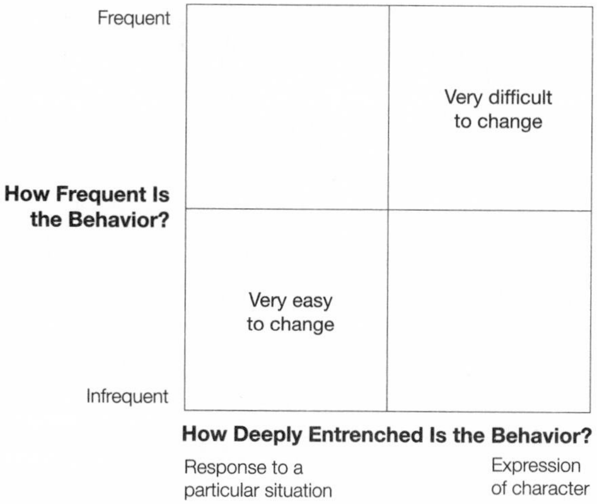

Source: James Waldroop and Timothy Butler, "The Executive As Coach," *Harvard Business Review*, November–December 1996, 111–117. Adapted with permission.

Ask the Employee to Prepare

Because coaching involves both you *and* your subordinate, both of you should prepare. It is important to involve your subordinate in every stage of coaching. One of the best ways of doing this is to have that person appraise his or her work performance. This is standard procedure for annual performance reviews. In many cases, the human resource department can provide a checklist for this purpose. That checklist should state the employee's goals and the job behaviors and functions associated with them. In self-appraisal, the employee evaluates his or her performance against stated goals. If your human resource department doesn't provide a checklist, here are a few questions you should ask employees to address in a self-appraisal:

- To what extent have you achieved your goals?

- Which if any goals have you exceeded?

- Are there particular goals with which you are currently struggling?

- What is inhibiting your progress toward your goals: lack of training, resources, direction from management, etc?

Each question will help you identify coaching opportunities. If the purpose of coaching is to prepare someone for a new job or a higher level of responsibility, the employee should compare his or her competencies against the competencies required by the new position, as in this example:

> Laura's boss thinks highly of her performance and wants to prepare her for a job with greater responsibility. He believes that she is ready, but doesn't want to push her if she has doubts about her ability to take on a bigger job. So he has given her a formal job description for a position he'd like her to consider.
>
> "Have you studied that job description I gave you last week, Laura?"
>
> "Yes, I have. It's very interesting."
>
> "Is there anything about the job that you couldn't handle right now?" he asked.

"Well, yes. This job would make me responsible for organizing and chairing weekly cross-departmental meetings. I suppose that I could learn to do that, but I don't have any experience in that area. I've never even run one of our own department meetings—where I already know everyone and what to expect. I'd be pretty nervous about running a cross-departmental meeting."

By asking Laura to evaluate herself against the requirements of a new position—and then listening to her—this boss has learned something he had not anticipated: her sense of being unprepared for one key aspect of the job. If he is smart, he will then give Laura opportunities to chair departmental meetings, and coach her to improve her performance *and* her self-confidence.

Self-appraisal by the employee has two benefits. First, it gets the person involved in the coaching experience. That involvement sets a tone of partnership for the appraisal process and makes the employee more open to feedback by the manager. Second, it gives the manager a different perspective on the subordinate's work and any related problems. Without this other point of view, the manager could make a mistake in judging the situation. Together, involvement by the employee and a fresh perspective make the job of coaching more targeted and more effective.

Preparation is a necessary prelude to coaching. It helps the manager to identify the causes of performance problems and forces the employee to confront performance and skill areas where he or she needs help. When both participants are prepared they are ready for the next coaching step: discussion.

Summing Up

- Preparation will make your coaching more effective.

- Preparation begins with direct observation, the goal being to understand the situation, the employee, and the employee's current skills and behavior. The insights gained from observing a coachee will enhance your ability to offer informed, relevant, and timely advice.

- Use observation to learn what an employee is not doing well. Then seek the causes.

- Look for performance gaps and skill deficiencies. These are your best coaching opportunities.

- Once you developed a hypothesis about a subordinate's problem, seek confirmation through someone else's observation—someone you trust.

- Listen carefully, both to what a subordinate says and what lies behind her words.

- Coaching takes time and energy. So pick only those coaching opportunities where you can truly make a difference.

- Some habits and behaviors are so engrained that they are not changeable through coaching.

- Because coaching involves both you *and* your subordinate, both should prepare. One of the best ways of doing this is to have that person appraise his or her work performance. Self-appraisal by the employee has two benefits. It gets the person involved in the coaching experience, and it gives the manager a different perspective on the subordinate's work and any related problems.

3

Discussion

Where Minds Meet

Key Topics Covered in This Chapter

- *Targeting observed behaviors, not supposed personal attitudes or motives*

- *Asking open-ended and closed questions*

- *Addressing the emotions behind the words*

- *Using discussion to identify the causes of performance problems*

THIS CHAPTER EXPLAINS the second step of effective coaching: discussion. If you are like most managers, you have a strong bias toward action. Your instinct is to jump in and start coaching. Resist that instinct for a bit. Instead of moving directly from observation to active coaching, you must pass through an intermediate step: discussion. This step gives you a chance to tell the other person what you have objectively observed in the preparation phase. In this step you will probe the other person's perspective. If you have prepared, you will be very clear about what you want to discuss—for example, Janis's presentation skills, Perry's store-window displays, or Oscar's handling of customer complaints. The discussion phase also gives the employee an opportunity to relate his or her view of where help is needed and the type of help that holds the greatest potential. Together, you'll be able to agree on performance problems and their causes as well as skill gaps and how they can be closed. And once that's done, the two of you will be ready for active coaching.

Discuss Your Observations

Once you are prepared, enter into dialogue with the employee about what you've observed. As you do so, stick to observations of actual behaviors instead of your suppositions about personal motives. For example, your coaching might focus on:

- A problem in submitting reports on time—versus "I think you're lazy."

- Too few sales contacts per day—versus "You must have a fear of rejection."

- A gap between an employee's current technical skills and the skills she will need to move into a higher-level job—versus "You're not up to the job."

One reason for dealing with behaviors instead of personal attitudes or motives is that behaviors can be documented with a high level of certainty; attitudes cannot. Behaviors are also external and disconnected from the other person's sense of identity. Finding fault with bad behaviors, then, is not an attack on his self-worth. Consequently, instead of defending himself, the employee can join with you in a detached and objective evaluation of the problem.

So, as you begin your discussion, stick to behaviors and begin with a compliment—that way the person will come away with his or her ego intact, as in this example:

> *"Harriet, I want to compliment you on your participation in last Tuesday's meeting with our sales reps. You had clearly done your homework—as you have done for other meetings I've witnessed. There is one area, however, where your participation could have been more effective—specifically, you interrupted Jane and Tony before either had a chance to give their views. I've observed something similar in previous meetings."*

Notice that the object of the manager's critique is a behavior, not Harriet's persona. Next, explain why the observed behavior constitutes a problem, and cite its impact on group goals and on coworkers, as in this example:

> *"Harriet, Jane and Tony had something to say, but we had no opportunity to hear it because you interrupted them whenever they began to speak. It's important that everyone has a chance to contribute. If they cannot, we won't learn from them. Worse, if one or two people dominate our meetings, the team spirit we've worked so long to build will be threatened. Do you understand what I mean?"*

When describing behavior and its impact, be truthful, frank, and supportive. Leave motives out of the discussion; doing otherwise will only make the person feel that he or she is under personal attack. Those motives would be pure speculation on your part in any case. Here are examples of assumed motives:

"You must have grown up in an argumentative household."

"Your habit of interrupting others indicates that you want to dominate other people."

"Your inability to get reports finished on time tells me that you don't like this type of work."

"Because of your difficulties with Mark, I can only assume that you have a problem managing male employees."

In the workplace, *why* people do things is usually less important than *what* they do. So don't try to play amateur psychologist. Instead, confine your comments to the behaviors that you and others observe. Then work toward altering bad behaviors and closing gaps between the performance you observe and the performance you'd like to see in the future.

But never lose sight of the fact that coaching is a two-way proposition. Once you've had your say, give your subordinate an opportunity to respond. If she is prepared, she is likely to respond with observations of her own. If her observations correspond to yours, you'll be well on your way to a coaching solution. If they do not, discussion of your differences is necessary.

Ask Probing Questions

The most productive communication between people takes place through dialogue—that is, through conversations involving two or more people. In dialogue, one person offers a proposition or asks a question and others respond, shedding light on the question, and often opening new avenues of inquiry. The iterative, back-and-forth of dialogue brings people closer to the truth. The dialogue method of inquiry goes back, at a minimum, to the classical age of ancient Greece, and to the Socratic dialogues written by Plato. The philosopher and his students used dialogue to pursue answers to ethical and moral issues.

Keep Your Prejudices in Check

Bosses form early impressions of their employees, and those impressions usually stick, even when employee behavior and performance change. This gives rise to the saying that "If management thinks that you're a genius, no amount of bungling on your part will change their mind—and vice versa." And there is some research to confirm this tendency to let early impressions stick. Jean-François Manzoni and Jean-Louis Barsoux have found that 90 percent of managers use their early impressions to segment their subordinates into in-groups and out-groups, which they treat very differently. For example, they tend to be open to an in-group employee's suggestions but ignore the suggestions of out-group personnel. Likewise, they accept the in-group person's mistakes as "learning experiences" even as they are highly critical of mistakes made by an out-group person.[a]

Do you have in-group and out-group employees? If you do, your attitude is likely to color the discussion phase of your coaching. Avoid this by all means. Maintain objectivity and a helpful demeanor in all coaching situations.

[a]Jean-François Manzoni and Jean-Louis Barsoux, "The Set-Up-to-Fail Syndrome," *Harvard Business Review*, March–April 1998, 101–113.

Probing questions are fundamental to effective communication through dialogue. They help you understand the other person and determine his or her performance issues.

"Have you tried _____ ?"

"What do you think is the best way to _____ ?"

"What do you think would happen if you _____ ?"

Probing questions like these open the door to effective paths of dialogue, taking you and the other party closer to the heart of the problems and their solutions. In particular, questions about observed behaviors help reveal underlying causes and suggest possible remedies.

"So you did try _____ and had disappointing results. Why do you think that happened?"

"I notice that you seldom share your views at team meetings. Why is that?"

"If you could replay that last sales presentation, would you do anything different?"

The coachee's responses to questions like these provide a springboard to still other probing questions.

Open-Ended and Closed Questions

There are *open-ended* and *closed questions*. Each yields a different response. Closed questions lead to "yes" or "no" answers. Use them to

- focus the response: "Are you satisfied with your progress?"

- confirm what the other person has said: "So, your big problem is scheduling your time?"

- keep both parties in agreement: "Then we agree that your current performance will not take you to your career goals?"

Open-ended questions, in contrast, generate participation and idea sharing. Use these to

- explore alternatives: "What would happen if . . . ?"

- uncover attitudes or needs: "How do you feel about your progress to date?"

- invite elaboration: "What, then, are the major problems with your on-the-job training?"

Use open-ended questions when you want to find out more about the other person's motivations and feelings, or when you want the other person to solve a problem for himself—that is, to talk his way to a satisfactory answer. Through this line of questioning you may be able to uncover the other person's views and deeper thoughts on the problem. This, in turn, will help you formulate better advice.

Tip: Create a Comfortable Setting

Many people are anxious about any discussion of their performance. So create a tone of partnership from the very beginning. Start by setting the person at ease; don't let the person feel that he or she is in the prisoner's dock. Then review the purpose of the discussion and its positive benefits for both parties. This will psychologically prepare you and the employee and will act as a "warm-up" for useful dialogue.

Do whatever you can to avoid interruptions by phone calls and other intrusions. For example, if you are holding a coaching discussion in your office, have all phone calls picked up by the voice mail system. Taking a phone call during coaching discussions sends the employee a nonverbal signal that the call has a higher priority—exactly the *wrong* signal.

Be an Active Listener

As a coach you must be highly tuned in to the other person. This isn't always easy. Many people are so confident of their views that they don't listen when others have the floor; instead, they use that time to prepare for their next statements. They pretend to listen but in reality are simply waiting for their turn to talk. You can avoid this problem through active listening—that is, giving the other person your undivided attention. By doing so you show respect and put him or her at ease.

An active listener pays attention to the speaker by

- maintaining eye contact;

- smiling at appropriate moments;

- avoiding distractions;

- taking notes only when necessary;

- being sensitive to body language;

- listening first and evaluating later;

- never interrupting except to ask for clarification; and

- occasionally repeating what was said, such as, "So if I hear you right, you're having trouble with . . . ."

Listen carefully, even when you disagree with what the other person is saying. This isn't easy. It's tempting to challenge statements you disagree with as soon as they leave the other person's mouth. Avoid that temptation. Instead, simply make a note of statements that conflict with your observations. Allow the other person to have his say, especially since you had yours. You can challenge statements when it's your turn to talk.

Listen for the Emotions Behind the Words

As you probe with open-ended and closed questions, be alert to the emotions behind the other person's words. An employee may say, "No, I'm not intimidated by the other people on the team. I don't speak up at meetings because I'm interested in what others have to say." But those seemingly confident words may mask a real fear of conflict with other people, or a fear that his ideas will be dismissed as weak or stupid.

As a coach, detecting the emotions behind the words may be your most important, but most difficult, challenge. Those emotions are an important clue to the kind of support the person needs from you. That support may take the form of:

- **Positive "strokes" that build up the person's self-confidence.** "Larry, you have the best intuitive sense of good design in our entire department. If anyone can learn to do this, you can."

- **Guarantees that reduce the person's fear of failure.** "I think you should try this. Yes, it's risky, but if it doesn't work you'll always have a position on my team."

- **Assurances that progress is seldom made without some conflict.** "So make a point of giving your views during these meetings. Howard won't like it, because your ideas conflict with his. But that's Howard's problem, not yours. In the end, healthy conflict generates progress."

Here the coach supports the subordinate's emotions even as she challenges him to improve and grow. Notice the tension in this. The coach will not succeed in challenging the person to step up to a difficult task if that person's emotional side is weak or unsupported. At the same time, the coach will accomplish nothing if she merely accepts emotions that stand in the way of progress.

Do you detect the emotions behind the words of your subordinates?

Have you done anything to support those emotions?

Are you challenging them to improve in the face of those emotions?

Tip: Create a Partnership Spirit

A sense of partnership in meeting the goals of the unit is important whenever you are reviewing an employee's performance. So, try to get that person to think about and talk about those goals and her role in achieving them. You want the employee to understand that everyone has a part to play in getting the right things done. You might even ask, "How do you think we are doing as a unit?" That's one way of making the person feel like a real partner.

Then ask the employee to talk about her self-appraisal. This will help you understand the employee's point of view and prevent you from controlling too much of the conversation. Listen very carefully. Don't interrupt. Hold your thoughts until she has had her say. Once the employee has laid all of her cards on the table, move on to your appraisal.

Move Discussion to Causes

People can and do change when they understand the consequences of their behavior and work. For example, you might say:

> *Our department's goal is to resolve all customer warranty problems within one week. That's our contribution to the company's higher goal of creating customer satisfaction and loyalty—both of which guarantee our future employment and bonuses. We can't accomplish that if any team member fails to handle his or her share of customer complaints. Do you see how what we are doing fits in with the company goals?*

Make sure the employee affirms your statement. Then move the conversation toward identifying the root cause of whatever performance needs fixing through coaching. "If you're falling short of your goal, why do you think that is?" Listen carefully to the response; give your employee the first opportunity to identify the cause. If you don't hear a thoughtful reply, probe with other questions: "Could the problem be that you need more training? Are there too many distractions in the office?"

Identifying the causes of performance problems will, in most cases, create an atmosphere of objectivity in which both you and your subordinate can contribute in positive ways. You won't be attacking the subordinate, and he won't be defending himself from your criticism. Instead, you'll be working together to address "the problem," which in most cases is *outside* the subordinate (e.g., lack of proper training, too few resources, the workplace environment, etc.) The following suggestions can help you offer more useful feedback:

- Encourage the employee to articulate points of disagreement.

- Avoid generalizations such as "You just don't seem involved with your work," in favor of specific comments that relate to the job such as "I have noticed that you haven't offered any suggestions at our service improvement meetings. Why is that?"

- Be selective. You don't need to recite every shortcoming or failing. Stick to the issues that really matter.

- Give authentic praise as well as meaningful criticism.

- Orient feedback toward problem solving and action.

Discussion is an important and necessary step on the way to active coaching. Use it to clarify your initial observations about your subordinate's performance problem or skill gap. Use it to probe for that subordinate's views, and listen carefully. By engaging the other person in discussion, you will also engage his or her collaboration in the next step: active coaching.

Summing Up

- Create a dialogue with your subordinate about behaviors you've observed.

- Don't be an amateur psychologist. Stay clear of suppositions about the other person's attitudes or motives. *What* people do is more important than *why* they do it.

- Iterative, back-and-forth of dialogue will bring you and your subordinate closer to the truth about performance problems or skill gaps.

- Use an open-ended question such as "How do you feel about your current progress?" to generate participation and idea sharing.

- Give your subordinate your undivided attention when he or she speaks. And look for the emotions behind the words.

- If your subordinate is falling short of his goal, move the discussion to the cause. Identifying the causes of performance problems will, in most cases, create an atmosphere of objectivity in which both you and your subordinate can contribute in positive ways.

Active Coaching
and Follow-Up

Getting Down to Business

Key Topics Covered in This Chapter

- *The importance of agreement on goals*

- *The benefit of having and following an action plan*

- *The two approaches to coaching*

- *How to give and receive feedback*

- *How to follow up*

ONCE YOU UNDERSTAND the person and the situation, you are ready to begin your coaching sessions. This is where the wheels meet the road. This chapter explains the business of one-on-one coaching, beginning with agreement on goals, and moving on to an action plan. It will show you how best to communicate and to handle feedback, and it emphasizes the importance of follow-up on coaching sessions.

Obtain Agreement on Goals

During the discussion phase, you and your subordinate should have talked about the goal of your coaching: to improve Lynn's delegating skills, to correct a problem in how she develops monthly reports, or whatever the issue happens to be. Now that the two of you are ready to begin active coaching, revisit that discussion and confirm your agreement on what the goals of your coaching should be. Make sure that you have a shared understanding. Make this the first order of business, as in the following example:

Well, Lynn, I'm glad that we could schedule this next hour to talk about delegating and how you can become better at it. As a new manager, you're surely discovering what I discovered years ago when I was in your position: that there is never enough time in the day. The only way to get your work and the work of your department done on time is to delegate effectively. Delegation also assures that your subordinates are kept fully occupied.

But before we get started, let's refresh our memories about what we discussed last week. My notes indicate that we agreed that it would be a good thing to meet for an hour or so every week to talk about delegating and to review your progress. You said that you would like to reach the point where you could confidently delegate three or four time-consuming tasks to your subordinates. Is that how you remember our discussion?

Notice in the example how Lynn's boss stated his understanding of the earlier discussion and asked for Lynn's affirmation. Notice, too, how he stated the benefit of achieving the goal: "The only way to get your work and the work of your department done on time is to delegate effectively." The person you are coaching must see a clear benefit in attaining the stated goal. At this point, ask for a formal agreement on the goal: "So are we agreed that our goal is to make you a better delegator?"

If the other person has different recollections about previous discussion or agreements, be sure to work things out. You must get to a point of mutual agreement on the goal of coaching.

Steps for Reaching an Agreement

Agreement is the foundation of coaching. You build agreement in the beginning as you commit to working together and throughout your relationship as you pursue the coaching objectives. The agreement process includes the following steps:

1. Inquiring into and advocating different perspectives

2. Presenting proposals

3. Checking for understanding

4. Checking for agreement

5. When agreement is in question, revisiting step 1 and beginning the process again

Create an Action Plan

Once you have reached an agreement, the next step is to develop an action plan that, through coaching, will produce the end you both desire. An *action plan* contains a statement of goals, measures of success, a timetable, and a clear indication of how the coach and the coachee will work together. The benefit of a formal action plan is that both parties know exactly what is expected, their mutual obligations, and how success will be measured. This eliminates the possibility of either party saying, "Oh, this wasn't what I had in mind" when the coaching program has ended.

Not every coaching situation requires an action plan. Many, in fact, can be handled spontaneously and on the spot, as in this example:

> *A subordinate handed his boss a spreadsheet with the second quarter 2004 sales results of each of the company's five sales units, arranged in column form. "Here's my first attempt at the sales report," he said, "I can have a finished version for you this afternoon."*
>
> *The boss glanced at the spreadsheet. "This looks good, but I'd like to make a suggestion. You can make your report more useful if you add two more things," she said. "For each region, add one column showing the quarterly sales from the previous year, and another showing the percentage change between this year and last. Let me show you what I mean."*
>
> *The boss then penciled in a column with the heading 3rd Quarter 2004 Sales and another labeled Percentage Change. "Do you see how that additional information would be useful to anyone analyzing our sales?" she asked. The subordinate nodded in agreement. "Now, do you know where to find last year's sales figures by region?"*
>
> *The boss went on to discuss numeric reports like this one, how the company's decision makers use them, and how comparative data help managers put business results in perspective.*

In this example, the boss didn't develop a coaching plan; instead she saw an opportunity to coach and did so on the spot. Notice how she complimented the employee on his draft before suggesting how it could be improved. She then demonstrated the improvement she had in mind and explained how it made the employee's report more valuable. That's on-the-spot coaching, and it is often the most effective coaching method.

Other situations, particularly those with larger goals, will benefit from an action plan. One clear example is when a subordinate must bring performance up to a higher standard within a certain time or risk dismissal. Another is a situation in which you are trying to develop a subordinate's skills to meet the requirements of the job or of a promotion. For example, consider the case of Harris, an employee who must be proficient in the use of the company's spreadsheet and presentation software before he can advance. In this case the action plan would most likely include:

- **A statement of the current situation.** Harris currently has only a rudimentary understanding of DigitCalc, the corporation's adopted spreadsheet program, and has never used CompuPoint graphic presentation software. The ability to use these programs for market analysis and presentations to management is required for advancement to an assistant market analyst position.

- **Specific goals.** At a minimum, proficiency will be evidenced by an ability to develop market segment data in spreadsheet form, convert that numerical data into bar charts and pie charts, and accurately communicate all data by means of CompuPoint presentations.

- **A timeline.** In their action plan, the coach and subordinate would agree on certain milestones of progress. For example:
  - By March 15, Harris will demonstrate proficiency with DigitCalc. By April 15, he will demonstrate proficiency with CompuPoint.
  - By May 15, he will develop a sample presentation using both programs and actual market research data.

- **Action steps.** Harris will use tutorials recommended by Mark, and will prepare a series of presentations using these programs and current market data.

- **Expected outcomes.** These steps and time-bound milestones lead progressively to full proficiency and promotion readiness.

- **The coach's role.** Mark Lange will meet periodically with Harris to provide coaching and critiques as Harris works toward his objectives. He will also provide Harris with technical assistance from the IT department if necessary.

Table 4-1 is a sample action plan you may want to adapt for your purpose.

Should the coach be the author of the action plan? Not usually. The employee should be given the opportunity to develop a plan to close any performance gaps. Say something like this: "What would you propose as a solution?" Putting the ball in the employee's court will make him or her more responsible for the solution and, hopefully, more committed to it. As the employee describes his plan for closing any gaps, challenge the assumptions of the plan and offer ideas for making the plan stronger. If the employee cannot put a credible plan together, take a more active approach. In either case, seek agreement and commitment from the employee to every part of the plan.

TABLE 4-1

Sample Action Plan

Problem: Employee routinely interrupts others during meetings.

Goal: A more collaborative approach to discussion during meetings; specifically, allowing others to make their points.

Timeline: By 4/15.

Action to Be Taken	Measure(s) of Success	Review
Employee will refrain from interrupting colleagues during staff meetings.	• No interruptions observed during two successive meetings. • No complaints from other staff members.	2/15
Employee will listen carefully to the views of others and respond with follow-on questions, not speeches.	• Number of follow-on questions asked.	After two more joint meetings with employee.
Manager/coach will comment on progress after each meeting.		

Source: Adapted from Harvard ManageMentor® *Coaching.*

Begin Coaching

As you begin coaching, communicate ideas so that the person receiving them can grasp and appreciate their value. For some people, this might be through telling: do this, then do that. Some people learn best through examples. Still others learn best when they work hand-in-hand with someone else. For an example of this last method, let's return to the case of Harris, who needed to learn the use of the spreadsheet and graphic presentation software. His boss, Mark, could have tossed a pile of user manuals on Harris's desk and said, "Study these. They will teach you what you need to know." Instead, Mark set up a projector and screen and asked Harris to take a seat.

> *I'm going to treat you to a slide show that Janice Bowman and I presented to senior management two years ago. It's our business case for the QuikPik product line that was approved, developed, and eventually launched last October. The presentation is based on market research data similar to the data you'll be working with if you advance to the market analyst level. I'll show you the same data in spreadsheet form after you've seen the presentation.*
>
> *Mark presented the 15-slide QuikPik case, explaining as he moved forward. Some slides summarized customer research findings in short bullet points. Others represented numerical market data in clearly rendered charts: market-share data in pie charts and forecasted cash flows in bar-chart form. Harris could see how the slide presentation, when coupled with Mark's narrative, gave company executives the information they needed to make a decision.*
>
> *"The reason I showed you this presentation," Mark said, "is to help you see the end result of good market analysis—namely, data arrayed in ways that create insights and communicate those insights to decision makers. If you want to be a market analyst, this is something you must learn how to do."*
>
> *Mark then went to his files and pulled out a folder of printed spreadsheets. "Here is the data behind the slide presentation you just saw. As you learn how to use DigitCalc, you'll see how you can take data like this and convert it into charts that help people grasp the data more easily."*

*After some discussion, Mark ended the coaching session. "Here's a
tutorial for learning to use DigitCal," he said as he handed over a
CD-ROM. "It will teach you the basics. What I'd like you to do over
the next week is to use this spreadsheet data to create bar and pie charts
like the ones I've just shown. That will be good practice. If you get
stuck, talk to Janice, who has agreed to help. She's a DigitCalc whiz.
When we meet again next week, we'll review your charts. I'll also have
some new market data that we can develop into presentation slides."*

Notice in this example how Mark communicated his ideas in a way
that Harris could readily appreciate their value. Rather than expect-
ing that Harris learn on his own through tutorials, he showed his
subordinate a complete example of what Harris should aim to
achieve for himself. He coached in a manner that made it easier for
Harris to learn.

What tasks are you trying to help your subordinates perform?
Have you provided them with tangible examples of good work or
good practice? Have you communicated in ways they can appreciate
and grasp? Your coaching will be most successful if you use a combination of telling and inquiry in your communications. Telling a person what to do and how to do it is usually necessary, and telling or
showing people how to do things is also effective and saves time. But
learning has a bigger impact when people figure things out for
themselves. So instead of doing all the telling, ask the other person to
tell *you* something with inquiries like these:

- Does what I've just shown you make sense?

- If you had to make a convincing case to a potential client, how
  would you use this software?

- Which of these charting formats would make the strongest impression? And please tell me why.

Inquiry engages the other person's attention and encourages problem-
solving behavior. But, as with telling, don't make inquiry your sole
form of communication. Effective coaches know how to balance
telling and inquiry. If you want to do the same, try following this
sequence:

Tip: Begin with the Easy Things

Some employees need coaching in several areas, which raises the question of where to begin. There's an old saying that we cannot learn to run until we've first learned to crawl, and then to walk. Mastery is, in fact, accomplished through progressive steps. This is true whether you are learning the martial arts, piloting an airplane, or managing and controlling a large organization. So begin with the easy things and move progressively toward more difficult tasks. This will reduce the risk of failure and prepare your coachee to attack more difficult problems with greater confidence.

1. Describe the individual's situation in a neutral way based on your observations.

2. State your opinion—your interpretation of what you have observed.

3. Make the thoughts behind your opinion explicit.

4. Share your own experiences if they might help.

5. Then encourage the other person to provide his or her perspective.

Overreliance on inquiry can result in the other person not receiving the full benefit of your advice. Conversely, if you emphasize telling too heavily, you create a controlling atmosphere that can undermine the coaching partnership. This balance of telling and inquiry assures that you'll make your point and that the other person will have opportunities to make his point heard.

Give and Receive Feedback

Giving and receiving feedback is an essential part of coaching—and supervision in general. This give-and-take of information should go on throughout the active coaching phase as the coach and subordinate identify issues to work on, develop action plans together, work on problems, and assess results.

Some people fail to distinguish between praise and positive feedback, and between criticism and negative feedback. Let's make these clear before we move on. Praise is simply a pat on the back for good work: "You did a very good job with that prototype demonstration." Positive feedback goes further, identifying particular actions of merit. "I liked the way you handled the prototype demonstration. The way you began with the underlying technical challenges, how those challenges were addressed, and finished with the actual demonstration helped us all understand the technology."

Criticism and negative feedback follow this same pattern. Criticism is a kick in the pants that explains very little: "That demonstration was poor. People in the audience were either bored or confused." Negative feedback, in contrast, brings in the details, providing a basis for discussion and improvement: "I think your demonstration suffered from a lack of organization. The good thing was that you showed that the prototype worked. But as a viewer I wasn't sure of the problem the prototype aimed to solve. Nor were the technical challenges made clear. Let's work on these."

Here are a few tips for giving feedback:[1]

- **Focus on improving performance.** Don't use feedback simply to criticize or to underscore poor performance. You should bring attention to work that is done poorly, but it is equally important to give affirming, reinforcing feedback on work that is done well—that helps people to learn from what they did right.

- **Keep the focus of feedback on the future.** Focus on issues that can be reworked and improved in the future. This means, for example, that if a subordinate's behavior or action was a one-time event, you might let it go.

- **Provide timely feedback.** Arrange to give feedback as soon as you can after you observe the behavior you want to correct or reinforce. Wait only to gather all the necessary information. On the other hand, if the behavior you observed was particularly upsetting, give everyone time to calm down.

- **Focus on behavior, not character, attitudes, or personality**. This will prevent the other person from feeling that he is being personally attacked.

- **Avoid generalizations.** Instead of saying, "You did a really good job during that meeting," offer something more specific such as "The graphics you used in your presentation were effective in getting the message across."

- **Be sincere.** Give feedback with the clear intent of helping the person improve.

- **Be realistic.** Focus only on factors that the other person can control.

Since coaching is a two-way activity, you must be as prepared to receive feedback as to give it. Without feedback from the other person there can be no communication. And without communication you cannot know if your advice is clear and complete, or if your coaching is even helpful. So encourage feedback from the coachee. "Is what I said clear?" "Is this where you are having the most trouble?"

When receiving feedback, give the other person your undivided attention. Provide evidence of your full attention by periodically paraphrasing what you understood the other person to say. "So, if I understand you correctly, you are not getting the support you need to get this job done correctly and on time. Is that right?"

Separate fact from opinion. For example, if someone says that your calculations are wrong, and then points out the error, that is a fact. If he or she instead says, "Your suggestion is unworkable," that's an opinion. Opinions should not be discounted—either yours or the other person's—but they shouldn't carry the same weight as demonstrated facts. So push back when feedback comes in the form of an opinion. Try to convert an opinion into specific information. For example, if the other person says that you have shown no interest in the coaching plan he developed, don't say "You're wrong. I *am* interested." Instead say, "What did I say or do that made you think I wasn't interested in your plan?" The same holds true for positive feedback. If your subordinate tells you that your coaching suggestions were helpful, ask for specifics. "How were my suggestions helpful to you?" "Is there anything more that I can do to help you with this problem?"

When you ask for clarification, do so in a way that doesn't put the other person on the defensive. Instead,

- be willing to receive both negative and positive feedback; and

- encourage the other person to avoid emotion-laden terms. For example, "You said that I am often inflexible. Give me an example of things I do that make you believe that."

And be sure to thank the person for his or her feedback, both positive and negative. Doing so will improve trust and be a model of productive behavior to the person you are coaching.

Tips on How to Get Feedback from Uncommunicative People

Some people are not very responsive, especially when they are being coached about a performance problem. Your attempts to solicit feedback may only elicit a perfunctory nod, as if to say, "Yes, I understand." But that isn't feedback, and it's no assurance that the person really understands.

How can you get feedback from uncommunicative people? Training consultant Nancy Brodsky of Interaction Associates, LLC makes these suggestions:

- Rehearse how you will respond if there is no reaction.

- Practice speaking slowly and taking long pauses.

- Make it clear that you expect a reply—and are willing to wait for one.

- Ask open-ended questions that help the person come up with a plan.

SOURCE: Harvard ManageMentor® *Giving Feedback.*

Adopt an Appropriate Approach

There are two basic coaching approaches, and you should adopt the one that best matches the situation.[2] In some cases you must adopt a direct approach. *Direct coaching* involves showing or telling the other person what to do; it is most helpful when working with coachees who are inexperienced or whose performance requires immediate improvement. Other situations call for *supportive coaching*; here the coach acts more as a facilitator or guide (see table 4-2).

Supportive coaching is especially important for those individuals who meet current standards of performance but need to prepare to take on new or greater responsibilities. With this group, be sure to:

TABLE 4-2

Directive Versus Supportive Coaching

Coaching Style	Used For:	Example:
Directive	Developing skills	Instructing a new employee who needs to develop skills in your area of expertise or matching him or her with another coach who has the skills needed
	Providing answers	Explaining the business strategy to a new employee
	Instructing	Indicating the most expedient way to do a task or working together with the employee on a task or project where she can learn from you; for example, a joint sales call
Supportive	Facilitating problem solving	Helping others to find their own solutions
	Building self-confidence	Expressing confidence that an individual can find the solution
	Encouraging others to learn on their own	Allowing individuals with new responsibilities to learn on the job, even if it means risking mistakes
	Serving as a resource to others	Providing information or contacts to help others solve problems on their own

Source: Harvard ManageMentor® *Coaching.*

- Recognize the good work they are doing. Without making promises, indicate that opportunities for advancement are available.

- Invite them to use their experience and expertise to coach others.

- Enter into realistic and open-ended discussions about career goals.

- Specify the knowledge, skills, and commitment required for different career moves.

- Ask them to describe the skills and knowledge they must develop in order to move ahead.

- Develop a mutually acceptable plan for acquiring the requisite skills and knowledge.

- Follow up on that plan at regular intervals with measurement and feedback.

Always Follow Up

Effective coaching includes follow-up that checks progress and understanding. This is the final step of the coaching process. Follow-up gives you an opportunity to prevent backsliding, reinforce learning, and continue individual improvement. Your follow-up might include asking what is going well and what is not. For example, Mark, the boss who was developing the presentation skills of Harris, his subordinate, followed up his initial coaching session one week later.

> *"Last week I gave you that tutorial for learning to use DigitCalc, our spreadsheet and chart-making software. Have you made any progress?" When Harris responded in the affirmative, Mark suggested that they use DigitCalc to create a set of pie and bar charts. "Here's a diskette with a DigitCalc spreadsheet file. It has market data on one of our new products. Why don't you open this file and show me what you can do with the data—just as you would if you were preparing a presentation for our marketing group."*

Follow-up sessions like this one are opportunities to check progress, praise progress, and look for opportunities for continued coaching and feedback. If an action plan needs modification, the follow-up meeting is the place to do it. So always follow up with these steps. Here are some of the things you can do

- Set a date for a follow-up discussion.

- Check the progress that the individual has made.

- Continue to observe.

- Ask how the other person is doing and what you can do to help.

- Identify possible modifications to the action plan.

- Ask what worked and what could be improved in the coaching session.

If you're a new manager, or new at coaching, your first efforts may feel uncomfortable and may not be entirely effective. Don't be discouraged. Don't stop. Instead, remember that you will get better with practice. So watch for opportunities to coach the people under your supervision, prepare yourself, and then jump in.

Summing Up

- As you begin active coaching, confirm whatever agreement you and your subordinate had reached on the goals of your coaching. Make sure that you and the other person have a shared understanding *before* you jump in.

- Make sure that the other person sees a clear benefit in your mutual coaching goals.

- Except for spontaneous, on-the-spot coaching, use a mutually agreeable action plan that will produce the end you both desire.

An action plan defines goals and measures of success, creates a timetable, and gives a clear indication of how the coach and the coachee will work together.

- As you coach, communicate ideas in a way that the person receiving them can grasp and appreciate their value.

- A combination of telling and inquiry is often effective in engaging the other person. Here, you tell someone how to do a task, then ask: "Do you foresee any problem with doing that yourself?"

- The two basic approaches to coaching are direct and supportive. Use the one that best suits the situation.

- Allow for feedback, from both parties—it's an essential part of the coaching process.

- Plan for follow-up on your coaching experience. Follow-up can prevent backsliding, reinforce learning, and continue individual improvement.

5

Becoming a Better Coach

Beyond the Basics

Key Topics Covered in This Chapter

- *Delegating coaching responsibilities*

- *Three conditions that improve coaching results*

- *Common mistakes made by coaches—and their remedies*

- *The challenge of team coaching*

K NOWING the *why* and *what* of coaching is enough to get started, but insufficient to make you excellent as a coach. Like many interpersonal activities, good coaching is often the product of personal qualities and interpersonal skills that cannot be taught in any book, this one included. Nevertheless, you can learn some things that will make your coaching experiences better. One is knowing when to coach and when not to. Some situations are better resolved through other means. Then, too, some coaching can be delegated, saving the busy manager lots of time and perhaps improving results. Delegating is one of a manager's most important tools, and there is no reason to believe that coaching, like other managerial chores, cannot be handled by competent subordinates in some cases. This chapter will help you to identify situations in which delegation makes sense.

You can also improve your coaching by creating a climate in which success is more likely. A hostile, adversarial climate is obviously not one that's conducive to the two-way participation required for effective coaching. Here you'll learn of three conditions that support coaching effectiveness. The chapter ends with a number of "do's and don'ts" observed by every good coach.

Conserve Time and Energy

Coaching consumes every manager's most valuable and limited resource: time. All managers are pressed for time: for budgeting, planning, hiring and firing, meetings, and the countless other things that crowd their daily calendars. As a result, you must be very judicious in the amount of time you allocate to coaching. Coaching is important, but so are many other things. Smart managers allocate their limited time in keeping with priorities

Know When to Coach and When Not to Coach

You will make the most of your time when you recognize that some situations benefit more from coaching than do others. For example, Rolf has a problem developing reports; they are excessively wordy, lack the heading and bullet points that make for faster reading, and never begin with an executive summary. His boss, Karl, is eager to help Rolf for two very good reasons: first, he has to read those reports, and second, Rolf won't realize his career potential without improvement in that area. But Karl knows that Rolf isn't even aware of the problem. Thus, coaching him might be a waste of time—time Karl could spend on something with a higher potential for benefit. He decides that the best course of action is to make Rolf aware of the problem and give him an opportunity to take care of it on his own.

Delegate When Possible

If you are an effective manager, you have learned to delegate responsibility for many tasks. Doing so gives you the time you need to deal with more important issues. It also gives those to whom you delegate tasks opportunities to handle more responsibility and develop their own abilities. Some coaching situations may be candidates for delegation. In some cases, someone else may be able to do the job, and do the job better than you. Consider the case of Rolf's report-writing problems.

"Rolf," says Karl, *"you did a very good job with those reliability tests. If you hadn't found those problems, we might have approved the current design and sent it on to manufacturing. That would have been a costly mistake. So thanks for that."*

After a brief conversation about Rolf's testing method and his findings, Karl brings up the report. "You managed to get all the important

information into this report," he says, holding up the document. "But can I give you a useful tip?"

"Sure, what is it?" Rolf asks.

"Make your reports more reader-friendly. Some of the people who read these things are simply looking for a summary—and they won't find it here—which means they won't read any of what you've written. Others are content to skim for key points and conclusions. And then there are a few technonerds, like me, who want all the details. Report writing that meets these different needs in a single document is an art. Unfortunately, it's not an art they taught either of us in engineering school."

"I know exactly what you mean," Rolf responded. "I'm never sure how I should report my findings. As a result, it usually takes more time to write the report than to run the actual tests. And if people aren't reading them, what's the point?"

"Exactly," said Karl. "So would you like some help on this?"

"Yes, I'd welcome it."

"Good," Karl affirmed. "For starters, I'll have you work with Sophia, a staff technical writer. Sophia isn't an engineer, but she speaks our language, and she has helped other people to improve their writing skills. I've already talked to her about this and given her a copy of your report. By the time she's through with you, Rolf, you'll be a prime candidate for the Pulitzer Prize in the report-writing category."

"I can't wait to begin," Rolf replied. "By the way, what's the cash reward these days for a Pulitzer Prize?"

Notice how the boss in this situation began with a compliment, then gained his subordinate's interest in a program of improvement. But in this case, the boss didn't suggest developing an action plan or a time when they might work together. Instead, he effectively delegated the coaching task to someone else—and to someone who had more to contribute.

How many opportunities do you have to delegate coaching to other qualified and willing parties? In some cases, your human resource department may be able to help with tutorial programs and contracted trainers. Remember also that you are giving the people to whom you delegate coaching tasks an opportunity to sharpen their coaching skills—skills they will need as they advance in their careers. Thus, delegation has three benefits:

1. It conserves your time and energy;

2. It provides personal development for one of your subordinates—the delegated coach; and

3. It helps the coachee to become more proficient.

As a final note, never forget this rule of effective delegation: The delegatee must assume responsibility for the outcome of the task. Thus, if Sophia accepts the task of coaching Rolf, she must assume responsibility for Rolf's report-writing progress. Accept the chore, accept responsibility for the outcome. If that sense of responsibility is lacking, the outcome may be disappointing.

Tips for Delegating Coaching Tasks

If you'd like to delegate some coaching, begin by making a list of the people who need coaching at this time, as shown in the following table. In a second column, specify the type of coaching required. And in a final column, list the people who are qualified to do that type of coaching:

A Delegation Checklist

Coaching Candidates	Subject Matter	Possible Coaches
Helen Andres	Laboratory procedures	Juana Sandoval Woodrow Murphy
Rolf Schmitz	Report writing	Sophia Parsons
Darlene McIntosh	Running productive meetings	Erik Jansen
. . .	. . .	. . .

Create the Right Climate

Another thing you can do to become a better coach is to pay attention to the psychosocial climate in which coaching takes place. Coaching results generally improve when executives, managers, and supervisors create a climate conducive to learning. That climate is characterized by

- mutual trust,

- accountability for results, and

- motivation to learn and improve.

Let's consider each of these characteristics in detail.

Mutual Trust

Have you ever helped a child learn to ride a bicycle? It is a scary experience for the child. She is trying to balance an unfamiliar piece of equipment and make it move forward at the same time. She knows that losing control or balance will send her crashing onto the hard pavement—and she already knows what that feels like. Reassurances such as "It's easy once you get the hang of it" or "Once you learn to do this you'll never forget it" are of no value to the child. The only reassurance that matters is the voice of someone she trusts saying, "Don't worry; I'll catch you if you begin to fall." The trust that grows from that reassuring statement will divert the child's attention of her fear to the skill she hopes to master.

Whether you are helping a child learn to ride a bicycle or helping a subordinate learn a winning approach to sales, trust matters. Trust has several sources:

- Expertise in the matter at hand. For example, the person you are coaching with sales techniques will trust you *if* you have a reputation as a successful salesperson. No one will take the advice of a known loser.

- Demonstrated concern for the other person's well-being and success. People trust those who demonstrate that they have the other person's best interests in mind. A good manager earns that trust by showing empathy for subordinates. When she asks someone to work late on a project she will also ask, "Would this upset any plans you've made with your family or friends?" Alternatively, she may say, "I know that this is an imposition—you have other things to do after five o'clock." Trust is also established when a boss demonstrates a genuine interest in a subordinate's career success. "I really trust my boss," Sheila told Max. "He's done a lot of things to help me move ahead, even though my promotion will create a headache for him." This type of trust is not the product of a single high-minded act, but by a habit of helping worthy subordinates expand their horizons and careers. It must be built over time through consultation, useful coaching, and by providing opportunities for the person to move ahead.

- Being as good as your word. Trust is built through repeated demonstrations that you are worthy of confidence. So, whenever you say, "Here's the plan: I'll do _____ and you will do _____," be sure to hold up your end of the bargain. And do it every time.

- Not disclosing information held in confidence. Discussions with an employee about a performance problem may inadvertently dredge up personal information that the employee would not want shared. Always respect his or her desire for confidentiality. And by all means, do not pry into the personal lives of your subordinates.

Build trust, and your coaching experiences will be more productive.

Accountability for Results

No one who isn't held accountable for results will take coaching seriously. Thus, the salesperson who doesn't see a connection between his performance and his paycheck won't take his boss's sales coaching seriously. He may politely listen and nod that "Yes, I understand what you mean," but his behavior is unlikely to change. Consequently, the outcome of his sales work will not change.

If you have a formal coaching plan, that plan should make accountability explicit. "I agree to help you develop your selling skills, and you agree to learn and apply them to produce higher sales." Whenever feasible, express that accountability in measurable quantities: for example, the number of sales contacts made each day, or the time required to process an insurance application. Improvements made in some tasks are less easily quantified, such as the conciseness and readability of a technical report or the quality of a presentation to the company sales force. Even so, a sharp manager can rate the "before-and after-coaching" quality of these types of tasks.

Motivation to Learn and Improve

Smart parents know that the best time to help their children master a new skill—be it riding a bicycle or tying their shoes—is when children are truly motivated to learn. Either because of peer pressure or because of genuine interest in mastering things that older children do, there comes a time when a child is both developmentally ready and mentally eager to learn particular skills. Attempts to teach them these new skills prior to that time usually fail. The workplace situation is very similar: coaching coupled with a motivation to learn is a powerful combination. Absent that motivation, coaching efforts are much less effective.

You are probably already familiar with the workplace motivations that encourage people to learn and improve:

- Mastering an important skill will open the door to advancement.

- An employee sees that improved productivity is reflected in her paycheck.

- A person knows that his job is in danger unless he closes an important performance gap.

- Peer pressure encourages everyone to do his or her best.

- An employee has reached the point where she is eager to learn something new or move on to a more challenging job.

These are the situations in which your coaching will be most effective and most appreciated.

Mutual trust. Accountability for results. Motivation to learn and improve. Create a climate in which these qualities are present and your coaching—and most of your other managerial activities—will surely be more effective. Are any of these qualities absent from your current coaching relationships?

Avoid These Common Mistakes

Few managers are great coaches. That should surprise no one, since so few managers are given any formal guidance or instruction in coaching methods—either in school or by their own bosses or companies. That lack of training results in several common mistakes. Consider these:

1. **Talking too much.** Managers are accustomed to talking and directing. Coaching, however, is a collaborative activity. The coachee must have an opportunity to talk about his work, where he's having problems, how he feels about his abilities, and so forth. A coach learns none of this when he or she dominates the conversation.

   Remedy: Resist the urge to talk, to tell, to direct in the early phase of coaching. When you do talk, make the most of your airtime with probing questions like, "What is holding you back?" or "How do you usually handle this task?" Alternatively, direct the conversation into an area where more information is needed for diagnosis; for example: "If you don't feel that you have enough time to develop these reports each month, tell me how you're using your time."

2. **Failing to listen.** Getting the employee talking won't do much good if you fail to listen carefully. Many people appear to be listening. They maintain eye contact and keep their mouths shut.

But they aren't really processing what they hear or looking for the elusive emotions behind the other person's words. Instead, they are mentally forming their next speech.

Remedy: Put all other thoughts out of your head as the other person speaks. If that is difficult to do, make a game of it: pretend that the other person is giving you clues to the location of a lost treasure. Do this and you'll hear and remember every word.

3. **Losing control of your emotions.** "Damn it, Smith," the boss fumed as he pounded his fist on the desk, "how many times do I have to show you how to do this?" Tantrums won't help your coaching. The only emotions that matter in coaching are those that support the coachee and make him or her more receptive to learning and improvement.

Remedy: Check your emotions at the door. If you are having a bad day or if you are upset by something, do something other than coaching.

4. **Directing the subordinate toward something he will resist without emotional preparation.** Chances are that you will encourage your subordinate to try something new or to reach for something higher, such as giving a presentation in front of an important client or group of senior managers. If that person lacks confidence, however, your encouragement will be a wasted effort.

Remedy: Prepare subordinates emotionally for the things you want them to do. If lack of self-confidence is an impediment to progress, deal with that fundamental problem before you push the person to take on an important assignment.

In amateur tennis and many other games, you are likely to win if you simply avoid making mistakes. The same holds true in the game of coaching. Avoid the mistakes described above and your coaching efforts will probably bear fruit.

Be a Good Role Model

Remarkably, the ultimate weapon in coaching may be your own on-the-job behavior. Your subordinates are watching you. They observe how you delegate tasks to them, how you communicate with the group, how you handle your time, and your personal approach to continual learning and improvement. And some subordinates pattern their own behavior on yours. So, if you want to be a great coach, be a great manager and fellow employee. Set standards you would want your subordinates to adopt.

Understand the Challenge of
Team Coaching

If your company is like others, many tasks are being handled through teams. Some teams are formed around routine business processes. A bank, for example, may form a team to handle sizable commercial loan applications. That team may include a sales-oriented loan officer, a credit analyst, and clerical personnel trained in producing loan documents. A team like this is usually permanent. Its members jointly schedule their production levels and work schedules, and may even have responsibility for retaining or rejecting people from the team. Other teams are formed around temporary or infrequent tasks, such as the development of a new product or planning the company's move to a new office building. This type of team brings together cross-functional skills and disbands once its work is done.

Whether they are permanent or temporary, the traditional boss-subordinate rules are suspended within teams, because you cannot obtain the benefits of a team and still have a traditional boss. A team has a leader, but a team leader is not a boss. He or she does not have the usual authority over others, and may even be outranked by certain members of the team. Nevertheless, the team leader retains coaching responsibilities.

In his book on team-based work, Richard Hackman states that good coaching helps teams in three ways: first, by enhancing the level of effort that individual members apply to their work; second, by assuring that the work done is appropriate; and third, by helping members make the most of their talents.[1] Good team leaders find coaching opportunities in the course of everyday business. Their coaching can help members with many routine activities: to make better presentations, to schedule their work, to deal with intra-team conflict, to obtain external resources, to set up a budget, or even to work effectively in a team environment.

Coaching opportunities are especially prevalent within teams because so many of the skills members eventually need are skills they must learn as their projects unfold. For example, an engineer re-cruited because of her technical capabilities may suddenly find that she must prepare and present a businesslike progress report to the sponsor and senior management. This type of presentation is outside her set of skills and experiences. She must develop presentation skills quickly—and coaching by the leader is often the best solution.

If you are a team leader, you can use coaching to help the others to:

- Rekindle motivation in the project

- Get back on track if they are having performance problems

- Maximize individual strengths (e.g., build on analytical skills)

- Overcome personal obstacles (e.g., reduce a fear of dealing directly with a difficult team member)

- Achieve new skills and competencies (e.g., learn how to make a better stand-up presentation)

- Prepare for new responsibilities (e.g., take charge of an ad hoc task force)

- Manage themselves more effectively (e.g., improved time management)

As in non-team environments, good coaching within a team produces greater job satisfaction and higher motivation. It may also improve your working relationship with other team members, making your job as team leader much easier and more successful. Just remember that effective coaching requires mutual agreement. The other person must *want* to do better and must *welcome* your help.

Practice Makes Perfect

Whether you are helping a team member or one of your direct reports, you will become a better coach by doing it often. Most of the things we all learn to do, from tying our shoes to handling other people, seem difficult and uncomfortable at first. Every new task has the elements of an experiment in which we try things and observe the results, good and bad. Even when our first efforts produce good results they feel awkward. Do you remember the first time you were in charge of a meeting? Were you tense? Did you have trouble keeping people focused on the agenda without acting like a drill

Doctor, Heal Thyself

You are doing lots of coaching of your subordinates. But what coaching do you need to be more effective or to move up to a higher rung on the organizational chart? Even the best managers need to sharpen their skills and knowledge. They might even benefit from direct training on coaching skills. At the highest organizational level—the level populated by CEOs, chief operating officers, and senior vice-presidents—people frequently need help with leadership style, the way they interact with their direct reports and other top managers, time management, and communications with key stakeholders. Do you need help in any of these areas? If you do, be sure to read the next chapter.

sergeant? Chances are that you grew more comfortable in your role and more successful in achieving your goals. Coaching is very similar. It is difficult and awkward at first, and you are bound to make mistakes. But it becomes easier with experience.

So practice your coaching skills whenever you have the time and the opportunity. There is no substitute for practice. Also, learn to coach in the moment. Not every coaching session must be planned. When you see an opportunity to help or demonstrate a better way to do something, grab it. Fast, on-the-spot coaching is often the most effective. By catching a problem in the making, you can prevent it from growing larger.

Summing Up

- Be very judicious in the amount of time you allocate to coaching. In some instances, you may be able to delegate coaching jobs to others.

- Pay attention to the psychosocial climate in which coaching takes place. Coaching results generally improve when executives, managers, and supervisors create a climate characterized by mutual trust, accountability for results, and motivation to learn and improve.

- Avoid common mistakes and your coaching will improve. Common mistakes include talking too much, failing to listen, losing control of one's emotions, and failing to emotionally prepare the coachee for what you want him or her to do.

- Coaching by team leaders is important but is made more difficult because team leaders are not traditional bosses, and should not behave like them.

- Like everything else, coaching skills improve with practice. So take every opportunity to practice.

6

Executive Coaching

When Bosses Need Help

Key Topics Covered in This Chapter

- *Why companies hire coaches for their executives*

- *Two different approaches to executive coaching*

- *Characteristics to look for when hiring an executive coach*

I F YOU ARE like many people, you go to a fitness center to keep in good physical condition. On any given occasion there might be ten to twenty people in the place, groaning at the weight machines or huffing and puffing on the treadmills and stationary bicycles. And there is probably one attendant, who keeps the place clean and, when asked, offers advice about using the equipment. She doesn't offer much in the way of programmatic advice or oversight.

Business tycoons and movie stars are also interested in fitness, but they don't mingle with ordinary folks at the gymnasium. Instead, they hire personal trainers to come to their offices or homes and put them through their paces. A professional trainer first evaluates the client's condition, talks about personal goals ("I want to get rid of this belly before my trip to Tahiti next month"), and develops a customized training regimen. He or she then monitors results and helps keep the client on track.

Senior executives likewise seek professional help when their on-the-job fitness is not up to their responsibilities. Executive coaching has a lot in common with the personal fitness trainer model. It provides a one-on-one, customized approach to altering behavior with the goal of improving on-the-job performance. And it has become a very big business. By one estimate at least 10,000 people are selling executive coaching services at anywhere between $1,500 and $15,000 per day.[1] At several visits per month over a period of months or years, the bill can get very large. But it may be worth it.

This chapter explains the potential benefits of executive coaching and the two basic approaches taken by today's practitioners.

Why Executive Coaching?

There are a number of situations in which executive coaching makes sense, but it often boils down to two basic reasons why companies hire coaches for their CEOs and senior executives: their behavior interferes with their responsibilities, or an executive needs to enhance his or her professional development through personal growth.

Altering Dysfunctional Behavior

Let's face it, some executives have personal habits that reduce their own effectiveness and the performance of people around them. Here are just a few:

- A failure to establish productive relationships with peers and subordinates

- An unwillingness to delegate responsibility and decision-making powers to their direct reports

- Placing the interests of their own units over the interests of the organization as a whole

- Resistance to collaboration with potential rivals for the next promotion

- An ineffective or inappropriate leadership style

- An inability to follow process in dealing with peers and the CEO

These are not fundamentally different from the bad behaviors observed in lower- and mid-level managers. But at the executive level they are more damaging to the organization. Thus, the people paying the bill for an executive coach may say, "This is very expensive, but if the coach can improve Charles's performance by just ten percent, it will be money well spent."

Promoting Personal Growth

Altering bad behavior is not the only justification for executive coaching. It can also be used to promote personal growth. Few people reach the executive ranks with all the knowledge, organizational skills, and interpersonal savvy they need to do an exceptional job. Most talented and ambitious people will acquire those capabilities through experience and learning. But until they do, they are liable to make mistakes—and mistakes at the executive level are costly. Thus, companies have a substantial interest in shortening the learning curve. Consider this example:

> *Sheila's resignation as Vice President of Marketing came as a surprise to everyone, and her departure created a void of leadership and direction that the company needed to fill rapidly.*
>
> *After an intense talent search, an internal candidate, Arvid, was tapped for the position. Arvid brought many personal assets to the job: He knew the company and its competitors, he was creative and strategic in his outlook, and he was a tireless worker. But Arvid had no executive experience. While his merits as an individual performer were proven, his ability to lead and enlist the collaboration of others was untested.*
>
> *"There's a risk that Arvid will fall on his face," the CEO told the human resource director.*
>
> *"I agree," she responded. "Even if he doesn't fail, it will take him a year or more to get control of his new job and begin making the contribution we need. This is a case where some executive coaching might be useful. It should reduce the risk of Arvid's failure and help him master the job more quickly."*
>
> *The CEO and the HR director agreed to hire an executive coach to help Arvid during his first eight months as marketing vice president. At a cost of less than 15 percent of Arvid's salary, it seemed like a good investment.*

Whether the problem is dysfunctional behavior or inexperience in a new role, executive coaching is often a realistic solution. It's costly, but so is the damage that some executives can inflict on shareholders. When companies figure that the benefits outweigh the costs, they hire a coach.

Two Approaches to Executive Coaching

Executive coaches, in general, follow one of two approaches. The first, which we will call "diagnosis and development," is the traditional approach. It has strong roots in psychology, is deeper in its method, but takes longer to deliver. The other, called "prescriptive" in this chapter, has more in common with the everyday coaching that managers give to their subordinates. It is faster and more direct. Each has its advantages.

Diagnosis and Development

The diagnosis and development approach to executive coaching has a great deal in common with the outside consulting model with which company executives are already familiar. This approach has four basic components: diagnosis, self-awareness, a development plan, and plan implementation.

Diagnosis. Like the manager coach methodology described in previous chapters, the consultant coach attempts to identify the executive's problem and its dimensions. This is done through direct observation, but also through indirect means, such as the Myers-Briggs personality assessment. In some cases, the coach will seek *360-degree feedback,* a method that systematically collects information about the client's behavior and performance from people who interact with that person: the client's boss, peers, and direct reports. The goal is to determine what it is like working for or with the client, and to identify strengths and weaknesses. Few companies give coaches the go-ahead to conduct 360-degree feedback, the reason being the many hours of consultant and employee time it consumes. In many cases, such feedback involves up to twenty company employees, who must take time away from other work in order to complete lengthy questionnaires. Critics of 360-degree feedback complain that most of the problems sought through this method can be spotted without that level of diagnosis. Adherents of the method, in contrast, argue that the executives being coached will take their problems seriously only if the evidence for those problems is objectively determined and clear in its meaning. The executive can easily ignore a coach who says, "You have a problem with _____." He can say, "Well, that's just your opinion, and you don't know me very well." If twenty people say that the executive has a problem, however, denial is more difficult.

Self-awareness. Once an assessment has been made, the coach meets with the client—often off site—to share what he or she has learned, both good and bad. The executive is brought face-to-face with his strengths and weaknesses. These sessions are bound to be emotionally troubling for the coachee since, as one writer put it, "There is nothing more disconcerting than meeting up with oneself."[2] The goal of this exercise is self-awareness on the part of the executive.

Development plan. Once the executive has come to grips with the problematic behavior or weakness being addressed, the next typical step is to create a plan to deal with it. As in other types of coaching, the executive is asked to play an active role in creating that plan. After all, he or she will have to live with it.

Plan implementation. The coach and executive work together in this final phase. The coach observes at close range how the client deals with subordinates, peers, and customers. Afterward, they discuss progress and problems.

> *"Let's talk about how you dealt with Johnson just now."*
>
> *"Okay. What about it?"*
>
> *"Do you think you delegated responsibility for developing a market survey to him?"*
>
> *"Yes. I told him what I wanted: a survey instrument of forty questions organized around five key issues, sample size of 1,200, and written in the format I prefer. What was wrong with that?"*
>
> *"You told him what to do, alright. But what responsibility did you delegate? You made all key decisions, leaving Johnson to type it into your preferred format. A secretary could have done that."*

This may sound critical, but that's what an executive needs to hear in many cases. The executive coach should be a truth-teller to his client, and point out correctable failings within the scope of the plan.

Naturally, implementation includes follow-up. Follow-up looks for positive change. For example, some executive coaches go back for a second round of 360-degree feedback. That feedback is shared with the coachee and compared to pre-coaching feedback from the same people.[3] If the coachee has changed successfully, the testimony of boss, peers, and direct reports should confirm it.

Prescriptive

The prescriptive approach is the alternative to diagnosis and development coaching. Coaches who follow this method do not spend nearly as much time on the lengthy and expensive diagnostic phase. Instead, they shadow their clients and prescribe new ways of acting as they observe the executive in action. Some critics say that this more direct approach is flawed in that it ignores the possibility that deep psychological problems are the sources of bad behavior. Marshall Goldman, a leading exponent of the prescriptive approach, dismisses this concern. "Therapy is certainly valuable for some types of problems," he stated in a 2002 interview with *Harvard Business Review*. "But it generally isn't relevant for the behavioral issues I work with. Virtually everybody I coach has reasons that are 'not their fault,' that make them behave the way they do. I just tell them, 'Let that go.'" Goldman urges his client to focus on what they can change, not on what they cannot. "When you're over 50, blaming mom and dad is weak. Can you imagine a CEO sitting down with people and saying, 'You know, I make too many destructive comments, and I analyzed why. It's because of my father.' Forget it . . . Grow up [and] take responsibility for your behavior."[4]

Whether executive coaching follows a diagnostic-development or prescriptive approach, it shares an important element with the day-to-day coaching that takes place between a manager and subordinates: The person must want to improve and make an effort to improve. As described by Marshall Goldsmith, "Managers who want to improve, talk to people about ways to improve, solicit feedback, and develop a rigorous follow-up plan, will almost always improve."[5] Consequently, the CEO who pays the fees and expenses of an executive coach

When Only a Shrink Will Do

Dr. Steven Berglas, a clinical psychologist who studies managers and workplace issues, has found that some executive performance issues stem from severe personality disorders for which psychotherapy is the only lasting solution. He cites narcissism as one example.

It is not at all uncommon to find narcissists at the top of workplace hierarchies; before their character flaws prove to be their undoing, they can be very productive. Narcissists are driven to achieve, yet because they are so grandiose, they often end up negating all the good they accomplish. Not only do narcissists devalue those they feel are beneath them, but such self-involved individuals also readily disregard rules they are contemptuous of.

Berglas makes the point that no amount of executive coaching can alleviate narcissistic disorders. Assigning an executive coach may even feed the individual's sense of self-importance.

SOURCE: Steven Berglas, "The Very Real Dangers of Executive Coaching," *Harvard Business Review,* June 2002, 86–92.

should be careful about which executives are selected for this type of treatment. Money spent on executives who already think that they walk on water may be wasted.

What to Look for in an Executive Coach

In the burgeoning world of executive coaching, practitioners come from a number of backgrounds: the senior executive ranks, organizational psychology, clinical psychology, management consulting, academia, and even athletics. Some specialize in different facets of management: career planning, organization management, time management, people skills. Whatever their backgrounds, look for these qualities when you hire an executive coach:

- **Business experience at a high level.** Executives generally prefer working with someone they can view as a peer.

- **Excellent interpersonal skills.** Look for someone who can work with big egos and not be afraid to address touchy personal issues.

- **Organizational savvy.** Because executives produce results through people and operating units, a coach must be adept at walking into a situation and quickly learning how the people and the parts work together (or fail to work together).

- **Personal integrity.** An executive must have the assurance that confidential matters will stay confidential. Caution: The executive coach's responsibility is to whomever is paying him. Thus, if the CEO is paying someone to coach one of her senior managers, that manager should know that the coach will probably be reporting progress to the CEO. However, the coachee's personal problems should not be shared with the CEO.

- **Frankness.** In most cases, being a good coach means confronting an executive with the truth as objectively observed. The coach should be capable of both empathy and truth-telling, no matter how disturbing that might be for the coachee.

If you hire a coach who brings these characteristics and good recommendations from previous clients, there's a good chance that you have made a good choice.

One thing to avoid is the "Svengali syndrome," or the exertion of undue influence by the coach over his client. Svengali was the villain in George Du Maurier's 1894 novel, *Trilby*. In that story, Svengali, a failed musician, used hypnosis to become the puppetmaster of a young singer named Trilby. Thanks to his hypnotic interventions, Trilby achieved great success, but at the cost of her own independence.

History records many counselors who enjoyed "power behind the throne" status, who, like Svengali, were seen by others as exerting undue influence over the leaders who employ them. Roman Emperor Tiberius had the ruthless Aelius Sejanus, who alone possessed his master's confidence. England's Henry VIII's *eminence gris* was

Tips for Making the Most of Executive Coaching

If you are the person being coached, your company is paying a bundle to make you a better manager. So view it as a great opportunity and make the most of it.

Management psychologist Don Grayson and consultant Kerry Larson have described six common pitfalls that prevent coachees from reaping the full benefits of executive coaching. They are:

1. Failure to commit

2. Unrealistic expectations

3. Defensiveness

4. Playing a passive role

5. Playing it safe

6. Failing to involve others[a]

As a coachee, you will make greater personal improvements if you avoid each of these pitfalls. So, be committed to the coaching process. Be realistic about what can be accomplished in a short time; behavior is not easily changed. Don't be defensive about the reason that you need coaching—don't make rationalizations or blame others for your failings. Be actively involved in self-evaluation and creating a plan for change. Take calculated risks in changing how you behave and manage; all advances involve risk. Finally, instead of hiding the fact that you are receiving help from a coach, be public about it and seek help and feedback from others.

[a]Don Grayson and Kerry Larson, "How to Make the Most of the Coaching Relationship for the Person Being Coached," in Marshall Goldsmith, Laurence Lyons, and Alyssa Freas, editors, *Coaching for Leadership* (San Francisco, CA: Jossey-Bass/Pfeiffer, 2000), 121–129.

Thomas Cromwell, who found traitors under every bed. The last Czarina of Russia, Alexandra, was much under the influence of the monk/mystic Rasputin. Each of these shadowy advisors was hated and eventually killed.

Executive coaches of CEOs must take care not to create the impression that they have undue influence over their client. They must not be seen as having a special relationship with the boss or special access that is denied to members of the top-management team. They must not be perceived as telling the CEO what to do or standing as a gatekeeper between the CEO and other company executives and employees. Their job is to help the CEO do his job more effectively.

Summing Up

- Companies invest in executive coaching to either alter dysfunctional behavior or to promote personal growth.

- The diagnosis and development approach has strong roots in psychology. Like consulting, it has four basic components: diagnosis, self-awareness, a development plan; and plan implementation.

- The prescriptive approach to executive coaching spends much less time on lengthy and expensive diagnosis. Its adherents shadow their clients and proscribe new ways of acting as they observe problems.

- When hiring an executive coach, look for high-level business experience, interpersonal skills, organizational savvy, integrity, frankness, and good recommendations.

7

Mentoring and Management

Developing Human Assets

Key Topics Covered in This Chapter

- *Coaching and mentoring: how they differ*

- *Three key benefits of mentoring*

- *Candidates for mentoring*

- *Mentor readiness*

I N Homer's timeless tale of Odysseus, Mentor was a faithful friend into whose care the world-wandering hero entrusted his son, Telemachus. Mentor's job was to guide the prince's development while his father was fighting in the Trojan War. Telemachus would be the future ruler of the kingdom; it was important that he be prepared.

Today, we generally define a mentor as a wise and trusted adviser. Consultant/author Chip R. Bell expands this definition: "A mentor is simply someone who helps someone else learn something that he or she would have learned less well, more slowly, or not at all if left alone."[1] And because the business world has no shame in changing perfectly good nouns into verbs, we now have the verb "to mentor"—that is, to impart wise and reliable advice, and a *mentor* is a person who helps someone else experience personal growth through learning. *Mentoring*, then, is the offering of advice, information, or guidance by a person with useful experience, skills, or expertise for another individual's personal and professional development.

This chapter will introduce you to the subject of mentoring: how it differs from coaching, its benefits and challenges, and its role in the development of human assets. Subsequent chapters will pursue the details of mentoring well.

Mentoring Versus Coaching

Mentoring aims to support individual development through both career and psychosocial functions. Kathy E. Kram first articulated these function over fifteen years ago, but they remain valid and useful today as we try to understand what mentoring is about. As table 7-1 indicates, the career functions of mentoring involve sponsorship, coaching, protection, exposure, and challenge. These are very much on-the-job activities; they aim to boost the protégé's capabilities and standing in the organization. Personal psychosocial functions, on the other hand, address the mentored person's inner self—his or her sense of how best to behave, workplace values, personal dilemmas, and sense of acceptance by the group.

Thus, the scope of mentoring is vastly greater than coaching, which is, itself, a small subset of mentoring. It is not limited to the development of some narrow set of skills or behaviors, but addresses the whole person and his or her career. As Kram writes:

> *Career functions are those aspects of the relationship that enhance learning the ropes and preparing for advancement in an organization. Psychosocial functions are those aspects of a relationship that enhance*

TABLE 7-1

How Mentoring Supports Individual Development

Career Functions	Psychosocial Personal Functions
Sponsorship. The mentor opens doors that would otherwise be closed.	*Role modeling.* The mentor demonstrates the kinds of behaviors, attitudes, and values that lead to success in the organization.
Coaching. The mentor teaches and provides feedback.	*Counseling.* The mentor helps the protégé deal with difficult professional dilemmas.
Protection. The mentor supports the protégé and/or acts as a buffer.	*Acceptance and confirmation.* The mentor supports the protégé and shows respect.
Challenge. The mentor encourages new ways of thinking and acting, and pushes the protégé to stretch his or her capabilities.	*Friendship.* The mentor demonstrates personal caring that goes beyond business requirements.
Exposure and visibility. The mentor steers the protégé into assignments that make him or her known to top management.	

Source: Adapted from Kathy E. Kram, *Mentoring At Work: Developmental Relationships in Organizational Life* (New York: University Press of America, 1988).

*a sense of competence, clarity of identity, and effectiveness in a profes-
sional role. While career functions serve, primarily, to aid advance up the
hierarchy . . . psychosocial functions affect each individual on a personal
level by building self-worth both inside and outside the organization.
Together these functions enable individuals to address the challenges of
each career stage.*[2]

Note: This book uses the term *protégé* when referring to the individual being mentored. The term's Latin origin (protegere) implies a
protected person or a "favorite." But general usage implies a person
whose career is being advanced by someone with experience or influence. The term protégé is superior, in our view, to the modern
business-speak: "mentee." We hope that readers agree.

The bottom-line difference between mentoring and coaching
can be summed up as follows: Coaching is about your job; mentoring is about your career. Table 7-2 identifies key points on which
coaching and mentoring differ in terms of goals, the source of initiative, focus, and other factors.

Consider the following example, which incorporates many of
the factors identified in table 7-2.

*Wendy is a laboratory scientist in the corporate research and develop-
ment unit of DrugCo Pharmaceuticals. She has a promising future and
is well-regarded by her boss and colleagues. Wendy reports directly to
Robert, who manages the testing lab in which she works. She also has
an informal mentoring relationship with Charlotte, an executive whose
responsibilities are in the area of intellectual capital and knowledge
management. Though she is not in Wendy's chain of command, Charlotte began her career as a technical specialist in the same laboratory
where Wendy now works. Consequently, she can easily empathize with
Wendy's career situation as well as the challenges facing a female scientist in an overwhelmingly male organization.*

*Yesterday, Robert stopped by to talk with Wendy about an interim
report she had just submitted on one phase of the lab's testing routines.
"That was a good report, Wendy," he began, "and I've passed it up-
stairs to Phil. I'm sure that he'll find it interesting."*

TABLE 7-2

Coaching and Mentoring: Key Differences

	Coaching	Mentoring
Key Goals	To correct inappropriate behavior, improve performance, and impart skills that the employee needs to accept new responsibilities.	To support and guide personal growth of the protégé.
Initiative for Mentoring	The coach directs the learning and instruction.	The mentored person is in charge of his or her learning.
Volunteerism	Though the subordinate's agreement to accept coaching is essential, it is not necessarily voluntary.	Both mentor and protégé participate as volunteers.
Focus	Immediate problems and learning opportunities.	Long-term personal career development.
Roles	Heavy on telling with appropriate feedback.	Heavy on listening, providing a role model, and making suggestions and connections.
Duration	Usually concentrates on short-term needs. Administered intermittently on an "as-needed" basis.	Long-term.
Relationship	The coach is the coachee's boss.	The mentor is seldom the protégé's boss. Most experts insist that the mentor not be in the other person's chain of command.

"I'm glad you liked it," she responded. "Did I cover everything you wanted in the report."

"Well," he said, "not entirely—which is why I came by this morning." Robert then spent five minutes discussing alternative tests that, depending on favorable results, would have strengthened the conclusions in Wendy's report. "Not that we have all the time and resources to conduct every possible test," he continued, "but in some cases they are worth the extra time and effort. So, if you ever feel that another test would clarify your findings, talk to me. I might be able to get you some extra help. In the meantime, keep up the good work."

Notice in this example that Robert's coaching goal was very immediate and limited. He aimed to improve one aspect of Wendy's job
performance. The coaching session was brief, impromptu, and initi-
ated by the boss. And it involved "telling" with feedback. While
sessions like this are bound to have a positive effective on Wendy's
promising career with DrugCo, the career issue did not trigger Robert's
intervention because *coaching focuses on the job, not the career.*

> *Wendy joined Charlotte for lunch later that same week. The two meet*
> *for an hour or so every month to talk about the larger challenges of the*
> *business and Wendy's career progress. Having started on the same track*
> *as Wendy with the same biochemical degree, Charlotte could appreciate*
> *the challenges faced by the younger employee and understood what she*
> *needed to learn as part of her career growth. For her part, Wendy had*
> *abundant respect and admiration for Charlotte. Charlotte had success-*
> *fully moved up through the ranks, first by expanding her technical*
> *know-how, and later by developing business management acumen.*
> *The M.B.A. degree she earned through several years of night courses*
> *had broadened Charlotte's perspective and had given her a toolkit of*
> *skills—achievements that Wendy admired and hoped to emulate some-*
> *day soon.*
>
>   *Charlotte typically began their mentoring sessions with a question:*
> *"So, what has Robert had you working on this month?" She would*
> *then listen intently to Wendy's response and follow up with another*
> *probing question: "What have you learned from that experience?" De-*
> *pending on Wendy's answer, Charlotte would offer advice on how she*
> *could build on that learning. In many cases, that advice directed Wendy*
> *to other people. For instance, one day Charlotte said, "A group of mar-*
> *ket researchers has begun meeting informally for lunch once a month to*
> *talk about changing customer requirements. At least two of those re-*
> *searchers came up from the science side. I think you could learn a lot*
> *about the business end of things from them. And they could learn a*
> *lot from you. Shall I introduce you to them?"*

Notice in this part of our example how Charlotte, the mentor, is
not particularly interested in job-related issues; instead, she concen-
trates her attention on Wendy's career progress via Wendy's learning
experiences. Thus, she asks what Wendy has learned during the past

month, and she provides a new opportunity to learn about the business by linking her with a group of market researchers—people with a finger on the pulse of the industry and its customers. Wendy will learn things from them that she will never learn through her laboratory work. This underscores what was stated earlier—*mentoring isn't about your job, it's about your career.*

The Benefits and Cost of Mentoring

The benefits of mentoring to the organization are threefold: (1) it develops the human assets of the organization, (2) it helps to transfer important tacit knowledge from one set of employees to another, and (3) it aids in the retention of valued employees. The cost of mentoring is measured in the mentor's time and commitment. Let's consider each of the benefits and the cost in turn.

Developing Human Assets

Now more than ever, and in most industries, human assets are of greater importance than physical and financial assets. Physical assets can be purchased, and financial assets are readily available in the capital markets. Neither differentiates the company that possesses them nor confers competitive advantage—at least not for long. Human assets, in contrast, are the source of innovation and value creation. These, in turn, differentiate a company from its competitors and have the potential to confer marketplace advantage. Thus, organizations have a powerful economic incentive to develop their human assets.

Consider the assets at your disposal: Which are the least expendable and the most difficult to replace? Chances are that you will answer "our human assets." Yes, you have offices and equipment; you may even own a manufacturing facility and a warehouse. But these physical assets can be replaced. Your competitors can copy or purchase the same or equivalent assets. You have financial assets as well: cash and marketable securities. But here again, financial assets cannot differentiate your company in the eyes of customers, and your competitors can acquire the same assets from investors and creditors.

The only thing that sets your company apart and gives it a competitive edge are its people and the things they produce: copyrighted materials, patents, services that customers value, a reliable stream of new products, and so forth. So you have every reason to develop those assets, and mentoring is one of the development tools you have at your disposal. Mentoring broadens an employee's perspective and gives people opportunities to contribute at higher levels.

Transfer of Tacit Knowledge

Tacit knowledge is knowledge that is difficult to codify and store in written or database form. It is the type of knowledge found in people's heads and nowhere else. Is there someone in your company who seems to know where every file is kept? Is there someone who always seems to know whom you should to talk to when you want to get things done? These individuals have tacit knowledge. A salesperson's awareness of who has influence and decision-making authority in a customer company represents tacit knowledge. Your own knowledge about how to get things accomplished in a team environment is yet another example. Though these understandings are difficult to record and make available to others, they are extremely important to organizations.

Mentoring provides a channel for transferring tacit knowledge from one generation of employees to another, or from highly experienced managers to those with less experience. In the absence of this channel, important information is isolated. And when the people who possess tacit knowledge retire or otherwise leave the company, that knowledge leaves with them. Mentoring helps to prevent that loss and to keep valued knowledge within the organization.

Retention of the Right People

Turnover is a fact of life for many companies, with the rate varying sharply between companies and between industries. The turnover rate for Southwest Airlines, for example, is between 4 and 5 percent per year—less than half the turnover rate in the U.S. air carrier industry. Southwest's turnover rate relative to competitors gives it important advantages in terms of recruiting and training costs, and greater on-the-job experience among its people. In professional advisory services, such as accounting and management consulting, the rate is huge: generally 20 to 25 percent! With so many investments in personnel recruitment, training, and experience going out the door, the economic damage caused by this level of turnover is substantial.

Not all turnover is bad, however. Turnover creates opportunities to fill vacancies with more qualified people. Turnover at mid- and upper levels also gives loyal and ambitious employees opportunities to move up. The challenge to companies is (1) to confine turnover to the ranks of low performers and among job categories that are easy and inexpensive to fill and (2) to aggressively combat turnover among high-value-adding employees. Mentoring is one approach to retaining high-value-adding employees. Its retention power is based on the following:

- Effective mentoring tells the employee: "We think highly of you and want to help you move forward in your career." That message tells the employee that he or she will not be left on a going-nowhere job plateau.

- Mentoring builds a personal bond and a sense of acceptance within the organization. When mentor and protégé are well matched, the employee is less likely to seek work elsewhere. Doing so would break a valued personal bond with the mentor and the organization.

- Mentoring enhances job satisfaction. An employee who has an effective mentor has the very real sense that she is learning, growing, and continually moving closer to her full workplace potential. That translates directly into greater job satisfaction and retention.

Translating the benefits of mentoring into financial terms is not possible. It may be possible to measure improvements in job satisfaction through survey methods, but taking it the next step—determining the financial savings attributable to higher retention owing to mentoring—is a long stretch. Still, intuition and experience tells us that the benefits of mentoring are real. This was confirmed in 1977 by Gerard Roche, then-president and CEO of Heidrick & Struggles, Inc., a management consulting firm that deals with executive human resource issues. Roche's survey of 4,014 executives reached the following conclusions:

- Executives who had had a mentor earned more money at a younger age, were better educated, were more likely to follow a career plan, and, in turn, sponsored more protégés than executives who had not had a mentor.

- Executives who had mentors were happier with their career progress and derived greater pleasure from their work.[3]

Mentoring Cost

The benefits of mentoring notwithstanding, it is not cost-free. Time and effort committed by executives to mentoring are resources that could have been spent on other work: planning, oversight of operations, budget control, talking with customers, and so forth. Is this an effective trade-off? That question can only be answered on a case-by-case basis and by the individuals involved. Many enlightened executives nevertheless deem mentoring to be worth the cost and view it as a natural part of their jobs.

Who Should Have a Mentor?

Which employees should have mentors? Some human resource people believe that everyone from the loading dock to the executive suites should have a mentor, but this is a minority view. Once the costs and benefits of mentoring are considered, it's clear that some people will not benefit—they are either not interested in a mentoring relationship and/or not yet in a position to gain anything from such a relationship.

Employees who stand to gain the most from mentoring include those individuals who have either moved up to a higher level, have moved into a new unit, or have recently joined the company. These people are in unfamiliar territory, which means that they may not understand the unwritten rules of the organization, or whom they can turn to in getting things done. Assuming that they have an acceptable level of self-awareness and an eagerness to learn, these people are good candidates for mentoring. Consider this example:

Flavio did very well as a branch manager of a national stockbrokerage firm. His stellar performance in the San Diego office has earned him an opportunity to move up to the position of Assistant Director of the firm's training department. This advancement will require a move to the firm's New York headquarters and put him in regular contact with key people in human resources, compliance, and sales. The job advancement will also require frequent travel to meetings with branch managers around the country.

Flavio will be operating in new terrain, have new responsibilities, and will meet with few familiar faces. Obviously, his boss must help him settle into his new job and become an effective assistant director of training. But his boss will be more interested in Flavio's job performance than in his career and his future with the firm. For these, Flavio needs a mentor.

For mentoring to be worthwhile, employees like Flavio should be "mentor-ready." Generally, a person is mentor-ready when he or she:

- **Is more career-oriented than job-oriented.** A job-oriented person is a 9-to-5 person who seeks satisfaction and personal growth outside the company. This person is unlikely to take mentoring seriously. A career-oriented person, in contrast, looks for satisfaction and growth in the workplace. To the extent that a mentor can offer career help, this person will place a high value on mentoring.

- **Has an appropriate level of self-awareness with respect to what must be learned.** For his or her career to move ahead, this person must have a sense of his or her strengths and weaknesses, and be able to envision a continuum of advancement and personal growth. He or she will view mentoring as one way of easing movement along the continuum.

- **Is eager to learn.** At bottom, a mentor's job is to expose the protégé to new things: skills, work experiences, people, and positions. A protégé who isn't interested in learning will benefit very little from this exposure.

- **Is ambitious.** The protégé must be eager to advance and take on more responsibility. In the absence of any one of these characteristics, the employee is unlikely to harvest the benefits of mentoring experiences.

Which of your subordinates are mentor-ready? Make a list. Do these individuals currently have mentors? If all do not, find out what is standing in the way and who would make a good mentor for them. And what about you? Is anyone helping you?

Summing Up

- Mentoring supports individual career development through sponsorship, coaching, protection, exposure, and challenge. It also addresses psychosocial functions: how best to behave, workplace values, personal dilemmas, and a sense of acceptance by the group.

- In a nutshell, coaching is about your job, mentoring is about your career.

- Mentoring has three benefits: (1) it develops the human assets of the organization, (2) it helps to transfer important tacit knowledge from one set of employees to another, and (3) it aids in the retention of valued employees.

- The cost of mentoring is measured in the time commitment made by executives to mentoring—time that would otherwise be spent on other important duties.

- Not everyone will benefit from mentoring. In general, the individuals who benefit the most are career-oriented (as opposed to job-oriented), are self-aware, eager to learn, and highly ambitious.

8

The Right Match

Advice for Matchmakers

Key Topics Covered in This Chapter

- *The characteristics of a good mentoring match*

- *The pros and cons of enlisting bosses as mentors*

- *Taking the initiative in finding a mentor*

- *Indicators of a successful mentoring relationship*

- *How one company created an online matching program for mentors and protégés*

NOT EVERY MANAGER or executive has the personal makeup to be a good mentor—to anyone. For one reason or another, these individuals simply don't know how to share, or are not interested in a mentoring role. Others have the right stuff to be good mentors to some people but not to others. Either they don't have strengths in a potential protégé's areas of interest, or there is not a good personal chemistry with the protégé. Thus, it is important to make a proper match between a mentor and protégé, and this chapter will give you guidelines for doing it right. It will define what is meant by a good match and how you can recognize a good match when you see it. And will address the pros and cons of adopting one's boss as a mentor.

What Constitutes a Good Match?

The benefits of collaboration are rarely captured in the absence of a good match between participants. A productive mentoring relationship depends on compatible personalities and complementary abilities and interests. So when you are seeking the right match, look for these characteristics:

- **Mutual respect.** The protégé must respect the mentor for his knowledge and accomplishments; the mentor in turn must respect the protégé for her desire to learn and for the good reputation she has earned within the company.

- **A logical fit.** The mentor should have knowledge or insights that the protégé seeks: for example, knowing how to build relationships with the company's strategic partners, or deep experience in developing innovative new products.

- **No political agenda.** The protégé's goal should be to learn. He or she should not attempt to exploit the mentor's organizational position with the aim of outflanking rivals for a promotion.

- **Compatible temperaments or styles.** An executive who has made her mark through careful, fact-based decision making might not be a suitable mentor for a rising sale manager who is accustomed to selling people on his ideas.

- **Commitment.** Both parties should be committed to the goals of mentoring. They must be agreeable to—enthusiastic about—investing time and energy in the relationship.

Bosses as Mentors: Pros and Cons

Many facets of the manager-subordinate relationship support the personal development we normally associate with mentoring. For instance, the boss understands the organization, its strategies, and goals in ways that can benefit the subordinate. The boss has a unique perspective: He has walked in the subordinate's shoes; he also has the political clout to open doors and move the subordinate into projects with the right learning opportunities. The boss also has a personal interest in the successful development of his subordinate: A capable subordinate can take time-consuming tasks off his shoulders, and he knows that he will have a greater chance of moving up if a capable person is ready to step into his shoes. These are favorable factors in the mentoring relationship, and they are not uncommon. Harvard Business School professor Linda Hill's research on managerial careers indicates that at least half of the managers she interviewed had past bosses who, though not mentors in the formal sense, had helped them though mentoring behavior. Two interviewees

remarked on how their former bosses continued to provide both
advice and counsel:

> *I turn to him for help now. He was the best boss I ever had. He set the*
> *bar high, more than any other manager I had. I trust him from my own*
> *experience. He handled me the way I wanted to be treated. He wasn't*
> *just interested in testing me; he cared about me [and] helped me grow.*
>
> *He calls me once in a while or I call him. . . . If I needed him to*
> *fight a battle for me, he would fight it. If I wanted to do something and*
> *he had his doubts about it, he would say, "Go back and think about it.*
> *And if you've thought it out, we will go for it."* [1]

There is a dilemma, however, in the boss–as–mentor situation.
The boss has evaluation authority over his subordinate. He makes reward and punishment decisions and he may be unwilling to help the
subordinate with career plans that do not benefit him (the boss) directly. Consider the following situation.

> *Philip, a mid-level manager in corporate engineering, has worked for*
> *Alice for the past three years. Alice values his competence and has no re-*
> *luctance in delegating important tasks to him. "I'd never get my work*
> *done without him," she tells herself. She also knows that her chances for*
> *a promotion will grow as management recognizes that Philip can step*
> *into her position as department manager and do a good job.*
>
> *But Philip's long-term goal is to move out of corporate engineering,*
> *which he views as merely one stop on his career journey. His aspirations*
> *are much larger and substantially different than his boss's. Philip enjoys*
> *talking with customers about their technical requirements whenever he*
> *gets the opportunity; he is also fascinated by the work done in the cor-*
> *porate R&D center. These are not activities that he can pursue to any*
> *great extent within the engineering department, nor are they of any in-*
> *terest to Alice.*
>
> *Philip gets along well with his boss but suspects (correctly) that*
> *Alice would not support his career interests. Consequently, he keeps*
> *those interests to himself and seeks out opportunities to make connec-*
> *tions with his peers in R&D and marketing.*

The example of Philip and Alice is not unique, but it is not universal either. Some bosses earn reputations as people developers who help others grow and advance in their careers. These bosses have counseling/teaching/nurturing personalities; they are truly happiest when one of their subordinates goes back to school for an advanced degree or is tapped for an important new position within the company. They see mentoring and career development as important aspects of their jobs. Mentoring and nurturing are in their bones.

Still, the boss's inherent conflict in being an evaluator and a personal guide does not go away, which is why most mentoring experts recommend that mentors be selected from outside the protégé's chain of command. As they see it, neither one's boss nor the boss's boss is a suitable mentor choice. This makes sense but creates a problem for managers near the top of the organization, where virtually everyone is in the chain of command. Who will serve as their mentors? Consider the case of ABC Manufacturing, whose organization chart is shown in figure 8-1. In this example, Susan is the Chief Information Officer (CIO); she reports to Kermit, the Chief Operating Officer (COO), who in turn reports directly to the Chief Executive Officer (CEO). Who would be a suitable mentor for Susan? Certainly not other executives at her level. Even the CEO is in her direct chain of command. That leaves only the Chief

FIGURE 8-1

ABC Manufacturing, Inc. Reporting Relationships

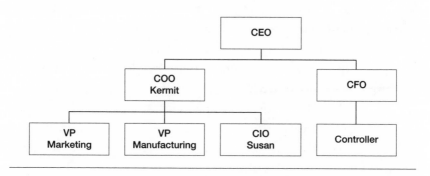

Famous Boss-Subordinate Relationships

Not all boss–subordinate relationships create mentoring problems, nor do they necessarily hold back the career development of the subordinate. Here are three noteworthy examples:

Tycho Brahe (1546–1601), the pioneering Danish astronomer, took on a young assistant named Johann Kepler. Kepler's job was to help his boss in making and cataloging precise measurements of celestial bodies. The two worked closely together for a number of years. Eventually, Kepler would use their accurate observations of the planet Mars to determine the fundamental laws of planetary motion. Today, science honors Kepler as one of the great physical scientists of the last four centuries. And Tycho Brahe, his boss, did much to advance his career.

President Thomas Jefferson was a mentor to his secretary, Meriwether Lewis, a young army captain. Each had great admiration for the other. Once Jefferson purchased French territories in North America, he groomed his subordinate to lead the expedition of discovery that would forever link their names. He sent Lewis to qualified experts, who taught him practical skills in navigation, medicine, and natural science. Thanks to his boss's help, Lewis and his co-captain, William Clark, earned a permanent place in the history of exploration.

Two decades after Lewis and Clark had completed their trek through the North American wilderness, university student Charles Darwin was in a boss–subordinate relationship with his Cambridge professor, John Stevens Henslow. A rising star in botany, Henslow made his office and home lively meeting places for budding naturalists. He led Darwin and other acolytes on botanizing forays through the fens and heaths of Cambridgeshire. And when a naturalist's place aboard the expedition ship *Beagle* appeared in August 1831, it was Henslow who urged Darwin to take it. "You are the very man they are in search of." Darwin took his mentor's advice, and his voyage aboard *Beagle* made his career.

Financial Officer (CFO), who may or may not have the right stuff to be an effective mentor to Susan.

Fortunately, people near the top are less needful of mentors; their career development is largely complete. As Gerald Roche has noted, "With rare exceptions, I have found that most executives view the first fifteen years of their career as the learning and growing period. That is the time when they seek mentors. By about age 40, those who are destined for the highest ranks are achieving positions of power themselves, and the need of a career sponsor fades."[2]

The Matchmakers

If a good match between mentor and protégé is an essential element of success, then who should play the lead role in bringing the two parties together? The answer is the protégé. Successful mentoring depends on the initiative of a person who says to himself, "I really need to learn _____," and then begins looking for someone who can help.

The ambitious learner is usually in the best position to identify potential mentors. This is done by asking questions like these:

"Who in this company knows what I need to learn?"

"Do I respect that person's competence and achievement in my area of interest?"

"Can I trust that person to be confidential and to act in my interests?"

Identifying a potential mentor is just a first step. The next step is to examine the potential mentor more closely. Someone must determine if that person has the time, the interest, the compatible temperament, and the desire to help the other person to learn the ropes. In a large organization, the human resources department is often in the best position to handle this second step. An HR staff person should approach the potential mentor, discuss the situation, describe the person seeking help and what she needs to learn at this point in her career, and ask, "Do you have the time to help this person?" "Are you interested?" If all signs are favorable, the HR person should then meet with the potential protégé to discuss the mentor's situation, and then set up an initial meeting between the two individuals. The HR person may wish to participate in that initial meeting to assure that the chemistry is favorable, and that mentor and protégé are getting off to a promising start. The HR staffer should then monitor the relationship from a distance. Consider this example:

Helen, a human resources staffer with career development responsibilities, was aware of Adrian's rapid progress in the production department. His stellar performance reviews and the praise he had earned from his boss confirmed his potential for greater leadership and responsibilities in the company. So Helen was not surprised when Adrian responded to the career development article she had written for the company newsletter.

"I read your article," he told her over the phone, "and I'd like to learn more about career development opportunities that apply to me."

Helen responded with a capsule description of the company's programs and inquired about his own situation. "Let me ask you," she began, "are you currently seeking career advice or guidance from other people in the company?"

"Well, yes," Adrian replied. "I am meeting periodically with Bill Sheffield and Shawn Williams. They are in different departments, and both are at the same level as me, but they generally have good ideas."

"I'm glad to hear that," she said. "Have you thought about having a mentor somewhere in higher management?"

"Yes, I have. There are two or three senior people from whom I know I could learn a great deal. But I don't know them well enough to ask for their help."

Helen saw her opportunity. "Perhaps I could facilitate that."

Adrian was pleased to take Helen up on her offer. The two of them met the next day, and Adrian gave her the names of three senior managers whom he thought would make good mentors for him. None were in his direct chain of command, and all had reputations for inventiveness and accomplishment.

As an HR career specialist, Helen was acquainted with all three of Adrian's prime candidates. She knew who were particularly practiced in developing the careers of their subordinates, and she also knew each of their organizational strengths and weaknesses. "Let me get back to you with more information in a week or so," she told Adrian. "Would you have any objection to my mentioning your interest in a mentoring relationship to any of these individuals?"

"No, not at all," he replied. "I'd be very pleased if you would."

Helen spent the next week seeking a suitable mentoring match for Adrian. She discussed the situation with her boss, the head of human resources. Both agreed that one of the individuals on Adrian's list would be the best choice. He was the mentoring type and had the knowledge and organizational clout that would benefit a protégé. Helen's interview with him confirmed that he had the time and the inclination to work with Adrian.

Helen set up a meeting between the executive and his potential protégé. The rest was up to Adrian.

Recognizing a Good Match

How will Adrian know if he and Helen have found a good mentoring match? The answer will be revealed over time in the attitudes and behaviors of the two participants. A successful mentoring relationship is indicative of a good match. Generally, you know that a mentoring relationship is succeeding when you observe:

- Enthusiasm and satisfaction on the part of both parties

- Interpersonal bonding

- Real learning by the protégé

- The protégé's increased self-awareness and self-confidence

Even a good match with these features cannot last forever. One party or the other's enthusiasm will wane. Or the protégé will say to himself, "I've learned as much as I can from James." These are signs that the good match is unraveling. When that happens, it is time for both parties to move on.

One Company's Matchmaking Experiment

Matching up people with appropriate and willing mentors has always been an individual endeavor. Ideally, people seeking a mentoring experience go hunting on their own; in other cases, they come to their bosses or to the human resources department and ask to be connected with an appropriate mentor—as in the example of Adrian and Helen above. The interconnectivity of the Web has created an opportunity to change this traditional approach to the "self-service" approach that so many Web sites use to connect customers with appropriate products and services.

Consider the case of Bell Canada, a telecommunications giant with more than 42,000 employees scattered over a huge geographic area. This company was searching for a way to transfer the knowledge of experienced employees to those less experienced and to break down the typical silos that divide the different business units. Mentoring seemed the best approach. But in so large and dispersed an enterprise, the company needed something else. According to Nancy Nazir, a company human resources executive, "What we needed was a unique mentoring structure that would be self-administrative, inexpensive to maintain, and easy for all employees to use." As she described to readers of *HR.com*, the company already had a traditional mentoring program, but that program failed to meet the needs of the enterprise as a whole. "It was limited in scope, relied on manual matching, and would have been too costly to implement across the enterprise."[3]

Bell Canada's solution was a low-cost online matching program designed to give protégés a way to browse an enterprisewide pool of potential mentors. That program was made available to all employees. The enabling mechanism was a search tool capable of generating a list of suitable mentors based on a protégé's own profile information. The benefit to users was its ease of use: A person needed only to describe what he or she was looking for, and the search engine would produce a list of people available to help. The benefit to Bell Canada, once the fixed cost of setting up the system was paid, was very low involvement by human resource personnel. Only a few hours of tending were required each month. That's the beauty of Web-based self-service in general, whether a person is shopping for a book on Amazon or a Volvo 240 on eBay's auction site.

Here's how Bell Canada's system currently works, according to Nazir:

> *Employees who are interested in being mentors fill out an online profile. Here we capture some key criteria about their backgrounds, which enables us to match their background to a protégé's preferences. So we captured, for example, not just work experience but location and language preference as well. . . .*
>
> *If employees feel they can benefit from this program, they can go into the Mentor Match portal and search for a mentor based on a variety of criteria. For example, if they are looking for a career in marketing, they could find someone with that background. . . .*
>
> *When employees go into the system, they are given a list of available mentors, who have been ranked based on their preferences. The employee can then click on each of the names to view the mentor's profile. Once the employee has selected a mentor, the system sends a note asking the mentor to look at the protégé's profile and either decline or accept the request. . . .*
>
> *If the mentor accepts, it's up to the protégé to initiate the partnership. At the first meeting there is an online agreement they have to sign. It's a one-year contract specifying the expectations and objectives for both the mentor and the protégé.*[4]

Once the year of mentoring is complete, Bell Canada's system sends the mentor and protégé an evaluation.

A Web-based mentor system like Bell Canada's is a low-cost solution for very large companies. Smaller organizations can accomplish something similar with manual sign-up sheets or pools of both protégés and mentors.

Low cost is nice, and so is its ease of use. But the system's value to participants must eventually be judged by results, which will be determined by the commitment of participants and the benefit they perceive.

Summing Up

- When you seek a mentor relationship, look for these character-istics: mutual respect, a logical fit, no political agenda, compati-ble temperaments, and commitment.

- A boss has a personal interest in the successful development of a subordinate, but his or her evaluation authority creates a dilemma. Thus, most experts recommend seeking mentors from outside the protégé's chain-of-command.

- The initiative for creating a mentoring relationship should come from the protégé. Human resource personnel can help identify individuals who have the time and the right character-istics to fill the mentoring role.

- A good mentoring match is revealed over time in the attitudes and behaviors of the participants.

9

Being an Effective Mentor

And a Receptive Protégé

Key Topics Covered in This Chapter

- *What distinguishes effective mentors from the rest*

- *Seven things that mentors should do well*

- *Being a good protégé*

A FEW individuals are natural-born mentors. Something in their own personal development has made them comfortable and effective advising others. Perhaps you know one or more senior people who have this special capability. Others need some practice and role modeling in the ways of effective mentoring.

This chapter has two aims. The first is to help readers to become effective mentors. It does this by identifying the personal characteristics and behaviors of effective mentors and by offering tips on how mentors should conduct themselves. The second aim concerns people who want to learn and expand their careers at work; it explains how they can be effective protégés.

Characteristics of Effective Mentors

Mentoring has many potential benefits: the development of human assets, greater retention, and the transfer of tacit knowledge, to name a few. Those benefits are only realized, however, when mentors play their parts well. So, what are the characteristics of effective mentors? A study conducted by Harvard professor Linda Hill during the late 1980s pointed to three characteristics:

- They set high standards.

- They make themselves available to their protégés—in other words, they are willing to invest the time and effort required for good mentoring.

- They orchestrate developmental experiences for those they counsel.[1] This is accomplished by steering protégés onto important projects, teams, and into challenging jobs.

These are critically important characteristics. But there are others; effective mentors also:

- Are successful and respected citizens of their organizations.

- Demonstrate good people-development skills—that is, they are good listeners, know how to empathize with others, and have personalities that make counseling and nurturing genuinely satisfying.

- Understand how their protégés learn best—for example, through discussion, direct experience, and other methods.

- Have access to information and people who can help others in their careers.

- Are candid in their dealings.

- Have good "chemistry" with their protégés.

- Are solidly linked to the organization—that is, they are satisfied and comfortable in their positions, and are unlikely to bolt to a competitor. The last thing a company wants is a role model/mentor who will leave, possibly taking bright young protégés with him.

This is a long list, and it's unlikely that you'll ever find a single person who embodies all of these characteristics. Yet many people fit this general description. Psychologists Timothy Butler and James Waldroop have described this type of person as one who has an embedded life interest in coaching and mentoring others.

For some people, nothing is more enjoyable than teaching—in business, that usually translates into coaching or mentoring. These individuals are driven by the deeply embedded life interest of counseling and mentoring, allowing them to guide employees, peers, and even clients to better performance. . . . People like to counsel and mentor for many reasons. Some derive satisfaction when other people succeed; others love the feeling of being needed.[2]

Searching for the Perfect Mentor

It is much easier to describe the qualities of effective mentors than to find individuals who embody them. In fact, the perfect mentor probably does not exist. This fact produces a problematic gap between expectations and reality. INSEAD professor and author Herminia Ibarra described this gap to readers of the *Harvard Business Review*. She was conducting a mentoring workshop for a professional services group and thought that a good way to begin would be to have protégés and senior executives describe their expectations. Their testimony pointed to a serious gap:

> *The protégés spoke first, enumerating the long list of characteristics their ideal mentor would possess. This person would be wise, successful, wield power in the firm, have extraordinary technical prowess, care about and have time for them, be a nice person, and manage their own life such that work wasn't everything. As the list unfolded, the faces of the assigned mentors showed increasing alarm. When the mentors first spoke, their words were candid: "That is precisely our fear—that you have expectations we could never possibly meet."*

Given that few people will meet a protégé's expectations of a perfect adviser, Ibarra's suggested remedy is for mentors to steer their designated protégés to a broad set of people and experiences until they find just the right person to work with.

SOURCE: Herminia Ibarra, "Making Partner: A Mentor's Guide to the Psychological Journey," *Harvard Business Review*, March–April 2000, 155.

You can identify managers and executives with an embedded need to counsel and mentor; you will know them by their behavior in the workplace and in the community. At work, they have a reputation for helping less senior people to expand their horizons and their careers. Outside the workplace, as Butler and Waldroop contend, they are involved in community service, literacy programs, and the like.

Who in your organization appears to have an "embedded life interest" in counseling and mentoring? How many of the characteristics listed above do they exhibit? If you are seeking a mentor, or planning a mentoring program for your company, these are people whose collaboration you'll want to enlist.

How to Mentor Well

Though some consultants and internal trainers are helping business executives to develop their mentoring skills, few people will ever come near any formal mentoring training during their careers. Nevertheless, if they do just a few things very well, their mentoring relationships will be much more effective.

Walk the Talk

Protégés look to mentors as role models of successful behavior. They learn as much, if not more, from observing their mentors than from what mentors tell them. So if you are a mentor, remember that what you *do* will make a greater impression that what you *say*. Furthermore, any perceptible inconsistency between your actions and your advice will send mixed signals to your protégé, creating confusion and loss of respect.

Give Actionable Advice and Feedback

Career development is a practical business. It has no other purpose than to produce good results. Consequently, your advice and feedback should point to things that are within the capabilities of your protégé. That which is theoretical or beyond the other person's control is a waste of time. Consider these examples:

> **Not actionable:** "Take it from me, someday you'll be able to lead that project team. You have good leadership skills."

> **Actionable:** "The first step is to become a member of an important project team. Even if your initial role is small, what you learn will help you assume team leadership in the future."

Not actionable: "If I were you, I would spend some time getting to know our key suppliers. As a company, we depend on a strong partnership with them."

Actionable: "You can learn an enormous amount about our manufacturing constraints by getting to know our key suppliers, Gizmo Products in particular. See if you can participate in a plant visit, or get to know Bill Johnson, the Gizmo representative, when he visits us."

Resist the Temptation to Solve the Protégé's Problems

A mentor's job is to help other people help themselves. Protégés won't learn to help themselves if you come to the rescue whenever they encounter problems. For example:

Jacqueline's protégé, Juana, has written her first formal report to senior management. In her eagerness to have Juana make a strong impression on top executives, Jacqueline crosses the line between advising and doing Juana's job. "This report needs heavy editing, and you should add a section on the pricing issue," she says. "Give me a disk version of your report and I'll make the changes over the weekend."

In this case, Jacqueline has made Juana's problem her own problem. Juana will be no wiser about writing formal reports than she was before.

Criticize the Behavior, Not the Person

When a protégé is going off track, the mentor has an obligation to bring the fact to his or her attention—not in a directive way, as in "Stop doing that," but in an observational way: "I noticed that you haven't volunteered for Project X; you might be missing an opportunity. Would you like to talk about it?"

As in coaching, it is always best to separate bad or inappropriate behavior from the protégé's persona. Doing so will prevent that person from feeling personally attacked and will make discussion easier and more objective.

Challenge the Protégé to Develop a Plan for Success

Never forget that the protégé is responsible for his or her own success. As a mentor, you are merely there to lend support and advice, and to open doors from time to time. If your protégé has the "right stuff," he will already understand the importance of planning. So challenge him to develop a plan for rising from his current position to one in which he can make a larger contribution to the organization. Say, "Where would you like to be five years from now? How do you plan to get from here to there?" and ask for a plan that includes the many learning experiences required to facilitate success. Then sit down with the other person and critique the plan in an objective way. Use your superior knowledge and experience to help him improve the plan.

Create a Foundation of Support

Like solid buildings, solid careers are built on strong foundations—of knowledge, ambition, *and* the support of other people. As a mentor, you are one of those "other people," but your support alone is insufficient. You don't know all the answers, and you don't control access to all learning opportunities. Your protégé needs support from many people. Part of your job as a wise and resourceful guide is to establish a broad foundation of support for the protégé within the organization and with key external stakeholders, primarily suppliers, customers, and strategic partners. Do that and your protégé will have a solid base on which to build a successful career.

Don't Allow the Protégé to Become Dependent on You

The best mentors put themselves out of the mentoring business by helping their charges to fend for themselves. There is nothing more satisfying to a good teacher than saying of his student, "She's at the point where she can teach herself." Conversely, there is nothing more vexing than a protégé clinging to his mentor's coattails—too afraid or unsure of himself to step off on his own. There are several ways to assure that a crippling dependency will not develop and that your fledgling protégé will eventually fly from the nest:

- Insist that he take responsibility for developing and following his own learning plan. Your role is to review the plan and suggest improvements.

- Don't give the answers; instead, ask questions. "What do you think would happen if you tried that?" "What alternative strategies have you considered?" "How do you think your boss would react if you did that?"

- Don't solve the protégé's problems. Instead, ask the person to discuss problems with you, then use dialogue to help the protégé find his own solution.

Get Off to a Good Start

Perhaps the single most important tip for being a great mentor is getting off to a good start with each new protégé. A good start is defined here as an open-ended conversation in which mentor and protégé get to know each other, establish rapport, understand each other's expectations, and identify a set of mutually agreed goals. Table 9-1 summarizes the things that indicate a good start. Most can be addressed in the first formal meeting between mentor and protégé.

Agreement on goals and responsibilities is particularly important. If these are left undefined, or if the parties see them differently, the mentoring relationship will be jinxed from the start.

Know When to Say Goodbye

In a 2001 radio interview, bluegrass banjoist Tony Trishka was asked about his most famous student, Bela Fleck. His teaching relationship with Fleck ended, he said, "when I had nothing left to teach him." Indeed, Bela Fleck had, at Trishka's hand, mastered the bluegrass idiom and had moved on to others, eventually creating his own unique blend of acoustic and electronic music with roots in folk,

TABLE 9-1

The Initial Meeting

	Mentor's Job	Protégé's Job
Come prepared	Learn whatever you can about the protégé before your initial meeting.	Same.
Talk about the big picture	Recount your own mentoring experiences to your protégé. Explain what worked and what didn't.	Listen and ask questions.
Discuss the protégé's needs	Ask questions and listen.	Explain where you are and where you'll like to be—and how mentoring might help.
Seek mutual agreement on goals and expectations	Explain what you can and what you cannot do.	"This is what I hope to achieve through this mentoring relationship."
Seek agreement on responsibilities	"I will do ____."	"And I agree to do ____."
Set a timetable	"Let's work on this for three months. Then we'll review progress and determine if we should continue."	Same.
Agree on meeting times and who will set them	"Check my calendar for suitable times."	"I will take responsibility for finding dates and times that fit into your schedule."
Insist on confidentiality	"Nothing we discuss will go outside this room unless we both agree otherwise."	Same.
Agree to be candid	"If this relationship isn't producing the results you expect, or if you disagree with my advice, say so. Neither of us has time to waste."	"I will tell you if this relationship isn't working for me. I won't waste your time."

bluegrass, funk, and jazz. And like every master mentor, Trishka continued to learn, resurrecting and performing banjo styles and compositions spanning two centuries. Both men continue to learn, innovate, and perfect their art.

The Trishka and Fleck example illustrates the temporary nature of good mentoring relationships. Mentoring is, after all, about learning, and both parties are bound to be on different learning trajectories that temporarily converge. The mentor has the wherewithal to provide guidance at one point in the protégé's course of learning, but must eventually end the relationship. This is both normal and indicative of good practice.

As noted earlier, a good mentor does not solve the protégé's problems or make her dependent. Instead, he facilitates the protégé's learning to the extent that he can and then helps her to move on to other learning experiences. "Your protégé now needs your blessing far more than your brilliance, your well wishing more than your warnings," says consultant/author Chip R. Bell. "Your kindest contribution will be a solid send-off. . . ."[3] The mentor should remain a trusted adviser, and may serve as a sounding board when the former protégé wants a second opinion on some new option. But his service as adviser and guide should be considered over.

Should the mentor follow up on his former protégé? Yes, says Bell, but not too soon. Give the protégé several weeks to find her way. Then follow up with a phone call or a lunch invitation.

For Protégés: How to Make the Most of Mentoring

The advice provided in the previous section aimed to help the mentor, but what if you are on the other side of the table? How can you make the most of your mentoring experience? In an article that advises professionals on how to make the most of mentoring on the journey to becoming partners, Herminia Ibarra describes a three-part iterative learning process. It may work for you equally well:

1. Observe different styles of behavior

2. Experiment with new behaviors

3. Evaluate the results of those experiments[4]

She notes that the up-and-coming young professional is likely to observe several styles of behavior among successful senior people: Some are aggressive, others are friendly and charming, still others are highly directive, and so forth. Each represents a potentially useful alternative. The person must then ask the following for each option, "Will this work for me?" "Do I want to act like that person?"[5] While it is tempting to say, "An aggressive style in dealing with clients wouldn't be right for me—that's not my personality," don't be too quick to dismiss a particular style; it may be useful in some circumstances. That usefulness is determined through the second step of Ibarra's learning process: experimentation. Here, one tries out different styles. For instance, the normally quiet young manager may experiment with being aggressive in some situations and highly collaborative in others. The final step, evaluating results, gives the young professional insights into what works and what does not—and in which circumstances. In most cases, success comes from adopting a range of possible identities, each one suited to a particular situation. Some may be more consistent with one's current personal style than others, but remember: your current personal style may stand between you and getting important jobs done.

A willingness to adopt a different operating style as one's duties and organizational status change is a bedrock of career success. This is often overlooked by ambitious employees. They, like many organizations, attempt to deal with change by perfecting the skills and behaviors that made them successful in the past, even though new skills and new behaviors will determine future success. Instead of expanding their range of talents, they become better and better at what they already do quite well. This is often a script for disaster. Consider this example:

> *Jocelyn has earned a reputation as an astute and perceptive financial analyst. She can track cash flows and interpret the numbers better than any of her peers. Her technical skills are impressive. She is also eager to advance to a managerial position. And she has many role models to emulate. Frederick, who began his career as a financial analyst, is a model of the competent organizational man; he works well with personnel from other functions in making decisions. Clarissa, another respected manager, has a marvelous gift for dealing with major clients and keeping them happy. But instead of observing and experimenting with those*

Tips on Being a Great Protégé
• Take responsibility for your plan of learning
• Respect your mentor's time and confidentiality
• Never insist on special favors that the mentor has not already offered
• Listen carefully and heed your mentor's advice
• Give back as much as you get

behavioral styles, Jocelyn has channeled her energy into further developing the analytical skills that brought her to her present level of success. Instead of preparing herself for a larger role, she spends her time in a pursuit of greater technical expertise.

Avoid Joceyln's mistake at all costs. Yes, technical expertise is important, but it counts for less and less as one moves up the career ladder. It is easy and relatively inexpensive for companies to hire technical expertise. What they need most—and are willing to pay for—are people who understand the strategy of the business and its challenges, and who understand how to produce results through others.

Summing Up

• Effective mentors set high standards, invest time and effort, and orchestrate developmental experiences for their protégés.

• Because there are few perfect mentors, career-oriented people should seek out a broad set of people and experiences.

• If you are a mentor to others, you should know that your protégés learn as much from how you behave as from what you tell them.

- Don't try to solve your protégés' problems; instead, help them to find and actuate their own solutions.

- Protégés should be responsible for their own developmental plans. The initiative must come from them.

- Establish a broad foundation of support for the protégé within the organization and with key external stakeholders, primarily suppliers, customers, and strategic partners.

- When you begin a mentoring relationship, set the ground rules during the initial meeting.

- Be prepared to end the mentoring relationship when your protégé is ready to move on.

- Career-minded people should be encouraged to observe and experiment with different behavioral styles in the workplace. They should then evaluate the results of those experiments.

Women and Minorities

Special Mentoring Challenges

Key Topics Covered in This Chapter

- *Tips for people who lack natural mentors*

- *The two-track system, and how mentors can help*

E VERYONE who has ambition and who wants to learn and expand a promising career can benefit from mentoring. Like Vitamin C, it's good for everybody and an overdose won't hurt you if the relationship between mentor and protégé is sound. But some people have less success in obtaining a mentor than others. Anecdotal evidence indicates that, in the United States at least, women and minorities of both genders find fewer mentoring opportunities than do their white male counterparts. Is this the result of some deliberate and malignant design to keep women and minorities out of the higher ranks? Perhaps this is true in some cases, but likely not in others. Many companies affirmatively seek out qualified women and minority job applicants. Some provide special counseling and career acceleration programs to keep these hires with the company and on the fast track to higher levels of responsibility. But the fact remains that people generally seek out and maintain mentoring relationships with people who are like them in terms of race, gender, and interests.

It is easier and more comfortable dealing with people who are "more like us"—whatever "like us" happens to be. Productive relationships, in fact, depend to some extent on a degree of identification, affinity, and trust between the parties. This penalizes people who have few potential mentors of the same gender or race, or who are reluctant to approach potential mentors whom they fear may not be receptive or supportive.

Consider the situation of aspiring female American managers. The number of women in mid-level management positions has grown substantially over the past twenty years. But to whom can these female middle managers turn for mentors in the higher ranks? Who is "like them?" In 2002 only 7.3 percent of line positions and only 6.2 percent of top *Fortune* 500 management slots were filled by women.[1] Thus, most potential mentors in these companies are men. Minority employees of both genders face the same situation, since so few minorities are currently in the upper tiers of management. And those that are tend to be in "soft" areas such as human resources, legal services, and customer service—the areas without profit-and-loss responsibilities from which few are chosen for top leadership.

Developing relationships across chasms of personal differences requires a willingness to take risks—for both mentor and protégé. The natural thing for most people in these circumstances is to hold back and keep the level of contact and engagement at arm's length. But this is bound to limit the benefit of the mentoring relationship.

This chapter addresses the unique problems of women and minority employees as they seek mentors and career development.

Challenges for Female Employees

In addition to the absence of suitable mentors described above, an ambitious female employee faces two hurdles in establishing a productive mentoring relationship: (1) the potential problem of a romantic interest on the part of the mentor, a situation that would undermine the entire business premise for the developmental relationship; and (2) the problem of balancing work and career.

As reported by Kathy Kram in 1988, both male mentors and female protégés report sexual tensions, confusion, and anxieties about personal intimacy.[2] This problem, which seems not to have changed greatly over the years, stems from the manner in which men and women relate to each other outside the workplace. This way of relating is carried over to the office, where it is inappropriate and antithetical to mentoring. Even in the absence of any inappropriate behavior, the female protégé can experience problems. Rumors may circulate, and ambitious male rivals may attribute her success in getting promotions and plum assignments to something other than merit. Some women may limit or forgo the mentoring relationship to avoid rumor or innuendo.

Different Networks for Different Genders

Because men dominate the upper tiers of business, aspiring male managers generally have the best of both worlds. The powerful male executives who mentor them on the job often double as social comrades—for example, at sporting events, dinners, and on fishing trips. This adds another dimension to the mentoring relationship. Up-and-coming women, says Herminia Ibarra, seldom have access to these same opportunities. Unlike their male counterparts, "female managers will often find themselves mixing with men in just the on-the-job network. This means that a whole set of executives will know nothing about them as people outside the office, a part of the equation that is an important factor for advancement in many businesses.

Ibarra observes that women on the fast track counter this defect by creating two different networks, each with its own objective. The first is the traditional on-the-job set of contacts, which in most cases is dominated by men. The second is a social network of women, both inside and outside the company. Ideally, each participant in this social network contributes something of value to others. "The idea is to . . . bring something to the table that you can broker for something in return," she says.

SOURCE: See James E. Aisner's review of Herminia Ibarra's research in "Nuances of Networking: Making Connections in the Workplace," *Working Knowledge*, Harvard Business School online newsletter.

There is also the problem of work-career balance. Despite the many changes in attitude about gender roles, women still bear the brunt of raising and caring for young children and keeping the homestead on an even keel. As Felice N. Schwartz once observed, "The majority of women are what I call career-and-family women; women who want to pursue serious careers while participating actively in the rearing of their children."[3] If the mentors of these women are men—and most will be—the odds are overwhelming that the mentors will be "career primary," that is, career will be the central focus of their lives. Pairing a career-and-family women with a career-primary male executive doesn't make for the best mentoring relationship. Both will find it difficult to identify with the other, and the mentor may view his protégé as insufficiently committed to her career.

A Different Fast Track for Minority Americans

Most large companies place their perceived future leaders on a "fast track" to the top. These individuals are generally paired with powerful mentors, given challenging assignments, and are expected to work exceptionally hard. Research by David A. Thomas reveals that there are two different fast tracks: one for aspiring whites and another for aspiring minorities. The fast track for selected white employees, according to Thomas, begins very early in their careers, whereas the fast track for minorities begins somewhat later, only after they have proven themselves over a number of years. "[C]ompanies implicitly have two distinct tournaments for access to the top jobs," he says. "In the tournament for whites, contenders are sorted early on, and only those deemed most promising proceed to future competition. In the tournament for minorities, the screening process for the best jobs occurs much later."[4]

The result of the two-track system, according to Thomas, is that promising minorities often grow impatient and sense that they are stuck on a career plateau. They become discouraged and demotivated when they fail to hit the fast track. They see others move ahead while they remain in the trenches. This may account for the inability of large corporations to retain minority talent.

What keeps minorities who ultimately succeed from giving up too soon, according to Thomas, are strong mentors. These mentors provide support in five ways:

1. The mentor opens the door to challenging assignments that build the protégé's competence.

2. The mentor places the protégé in a position of trust that helps build self-confidence and credibility for the individual within the organization.

Tips for Women and Minorities

If you are a woman or a minority employee, here are some things you can do to obtain mentoring help:

- Don't bank on a single mentor to help you learn and to open doors. Instead, develop a network of mentors and supporters. Together, they will find ways to steer you into valuable assignments and back you up when you need help. A 1997 study of managers by Herminia Ibarra, for instance, found that having a mentor matters less than having a wide mix of professional contacts—contacts that include both men and women.

- Be very careful about the assignments you accept or for which you volunteer. Latch onto assignments that challenge your skills and give you visibility. Avoid assignments that are easy or that will not be noticed by senior management.

- Given a choice between a staff position and one with profit-and-loss responsibility, take the latter unless there is a compelling reason to do otherwise. Positions with P&L responsibility will expose you to a more critical set of demands, decisions, and management development—the kind that opens more doors to advancement.

- Find satisfaction in personal growth, even if it is not immediately rewarded. As long as you know that you are learning and building your competencies, tell yourself "This is working."

- Use time in the learning trenches to develop self-confidence, technical competence, and credibility among your peers and senior management.

- Work on your perceived image. Find an image that matches well with the organization's culture.

3. The mentor's advice keeps the protégé on the right track; he or she will not take aimless detours into assignments that will not produce career benefits.

4. In later years, the mentor sponsors the protégé for important new positions.

5. The mentor confronts those who are hostile to the protégé on racial, gender, or ethnic grounds.[5]

There is no doubt that women and minorities generally face a more challenging road to the top. This is changing gradually as an earlier echelon of aspiring women and minority managers has moved from the lower to the middle ranks. Some of these individuals are reaching the higher rungs of the ladder, and as they do so they are becoming useful mentors for the next wave. But until their numbers at the top increase, women and minorities must work harder and smarter in establishing good mentoring relationships.

Summing Up

- In the United States, women and minorities of both genders find fewer mentoring opportunities than do their white male counterparts.

- People generally seek out and maintain mentoring relationships with people who are like them in terms of race, gender, and interests.

- Aspiring employees who cannot find a natural mentor should develop a network of mentors and supporters.

Beyond Traditional Mentoring

Peers and Networks

Key Topics Covered in This Chapter

- *Learning from peers*

- *When peer mentoring works best*

- *The benefits of a mentoring network*

- *Tips for creating a network of mentors*

PREVIOUS CHAPTERS on mentoring have focused on the traditional approach, in which a higher-ranking, more experienced manager or executive provides guidance and sage advice to a lower-ranking, less experienced protégé. This one-on-one approach of master and apprentice has much to recommend it. However, that approach has no monopoly on the career and psychosocial functions that people seek in mentoring relationships, specifically:

- Sponsorship that opens doors

- Coaching

- A measure of organizational protection

- Opportunities for greater visibility in the company

- Challenging assignments that stretch one's capabilities

- Role modeling of appropriate behaviors and values

- Counseling

- Support and acceptance

- Friendship that makes one feel secure and appreciated.[1]

Some of these functions can be obtained through peer-to-peer mentoring, and all can be captured through a mentoring network that includes both peers and higher-level people. This chapter will explore these nontraditional approaches to mentoring and how you can make the most of them.

Mentoring Peer–to–Peer

The value of peer-to-peer mentoring has been documented in Linda Hill's 1992 study of newly minted managers.[2] Most of the managers in that study testified that access to a network of peers was a key ingredient in their successful mentoring experiences. In the end, they judged relationships with peers—and not with superiors—to be their most important developmental experiences.

Peer-to-peer mentoring rests on this solid premise: Ambitious and hardworking young managers have a great deal to learn from each other, and because they have shared experiences, they can empathize and provide mutual support.

Patrick, a twenty-something market analyst, has a problem. His boss gives him almost no opportunities to make decisions or to make larger contributions to the marketing department. As he explains to his friend, Bob, a peer in the logistics department, and a person with whom Patrick has worked frequently, "I like my boss as a person, and we generally get along well, but he's driving me crazy."

"What do you mean?" Bob asks.

"Well, he's a 'do this, do that' type of boss. He makes all the plans and even plans out my week. I'm almost never consulted about what we are doing. I'm never going to learn anything or gain visibility in this company if this continues. This is really frustrating."

Bob thinks for a moment. "Have you talked to him about this?"

"Yes, several times," Patrick replies dejectedly. "But it doesn't register. The next day he has another to-do list for me."

Bob agrees that Patrick has a big problem—one that might retard his career. "You have a lot to contribute," Bob says. "What you need are opportunities for doing it."

They talk about various options: hope that the boss will either move or get fired (not likely); talk confidentially to someone in human resources about the problem (more promising); or look for opportunities elsewhere (why not, Patrick has nothing to lose).

"I have one more idea," Bob says. "I'm having lunch next Monday with Bert Malloy. Bert's a marketing guy with PartsCo, one of our key suppliers. I work with him often. He's about five years older than

us, smart, a guy you can trust with confidential information, and he's had lots of management experience—a lot more than either of us. Why don't you join us for lunch? Bert might have some ideas for you. Who knows, he might offer you a job!"

In this story, Bob plays the role of mentoring peer. He provides several of the functions associated with traditional mentoring: counseling, acceptance, and friendship. And in putting Patrick in touch with Bert, he may have opened the door to additional counseling, role modeling, and exposure to new career opportunities.

Drawbacks

Peer mentors have drawbacks. They lack the power of high-level mentors, which means that they cannot provide the sponsorship, protection, challenge (through new assignments), and role modeling that many people need. Peers may also be competitors for promotions, resources, and the favor of senior management. That competitive element may undermine the trust that mentoring relationships require. Also, some individuals may be reluctant to admit to a competitive peer that they need help. Doing so says, "You're the master and I'm the apprentice. You are better than me." Not many people will say this to a peer.

Advantages

Despite the obvious disadvantages, mentoring peers have two factors in their favor:

- There are usually many more peer mentors than senior mentors to choose from in a large company. Once all the direct bosses and chain-of-command executives are eliminated from the mentoring pool, there are few people left to turn to for help and advice. And those that do remain may lack the particular experiences or skills that the protégé seeks. Some may be real losers who got to the top through seniority or a sycophantic relationship with a higher-up. In contrast, the typical young manager has many peers to whom he can turn for advice.

- A peer is more likely to understand and empathize with the problems of the ambitious, young learner. He or she is, after all, in a very similar situation.

Peer mentoring works best when (1) peers agree that each has something to learn from the other, (2) when confidentiality can be maintained, and (3) when each is willing to reciprocate. Consider this example:

> *Andrea is a new employee who brings exceptional experience in dealing productively with strategic partners. Her main weakness is her ignorance of the unwritten rules of how to get things done in the company. Brad, on the other hand, has been around for several years and is an accomplished networker. He knows whom to call to get things done. But Brad has no experience in dealing with outsiders—something he must learn to do well if he hopes to advance within the company.*

Andrea and Brad have a basis to be peer mentors. Each has something of value for the other. Some companies attempt to match people like Andrea and Brad in one-on-one peer mentoring relationships (see figure 11-1). In most cases the human resources department is in a good position to play this matchmaking role.

A more ambitious approach to peer mentoring is to create a formal pool of mentoring peers, as described in figure 11-2. Here the

FIGURE 11-1

A One-on-One Mentoring Relationship

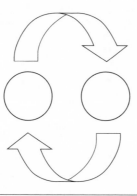

HR department determines which special capability each person has to contribute to the pool, and which capability each could use in developing his or her career. One company, for example, decided to pursue the seven habits of highly effective people described in Stephen R. Covey's best-selling book of the same name. The company's human resource department took the lead in identifying individuals who had the greatest apparent mastery of each of the seven habits. These individuals were then asked to coach a group of peers on those habits.

Each participant in this type of arrangement contributes to the pool, and each draws a share of learning from it. The drawbacks of the mentoring pool are twofold: (1) it requires substantial coordination, and (2) it shifts the initiative from individual learners to the human resource department, which fills the coordinating role.

In the end, peer mentoring—either one-on-one or pooled—is a mixed bag of advantages and disadvantages, but one that can be as useful as any you will establish with a high-level individual. If you

FIGURE 11-2

A Mentoring Pool

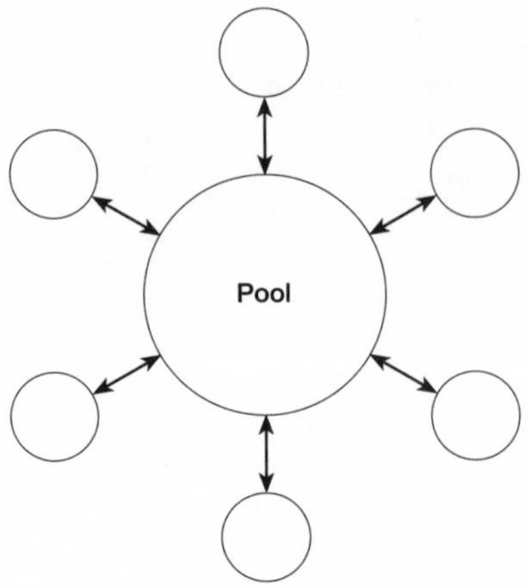

are seeking mentoring through this channel, be judicious about the people you approach for help. Look for individuals who have an important workplace quality you lack, and who are not intense competitors for the positions you seek. And above all, look for people you can trust.

Network Mentoring

Chopin once said, "Nothing is more beautiful than a guitar, except, possibly, two." Yes, more of some things is better than less, and that applies to mentors. If there is one form of support and learning with greater potential for the development of ambitious managers than the master-protégé and peer-to-peer models described earlier, it is a network of many mentors. Linda Hill, in the same research cited earlier in this chapter, also found that those who reported extensive and varied networks of advisors and contacts, and who were willing to ask for help, had an easier time coping with their initial management challenges. As one budding manager told her:

> As I saw what an opportunity for learning it was to talk to as wide a range of people as I could, I got better at calling up managers around the country and getting to the point. I'd admit I was just looking for new ideas. "Here is a situation. What would you do in this situation?" . . .
>
> I don't think you need just one mentor. You need to have lots of people you can turn to for advice. You need to have friends who are experts about different things. [3]

Many individuals in Hill's study, like the one cited above, reported that they contacted peers in their networks on a weekly basis.

The benefits of a strong mentoring network are many:

- A "diversified portfolio" of mentors is more able than a single mentor to provide the spectrum of career and psychosocial functions required by the upwardly mobile manager. A single mentor can open some doors but not others. He or she can model some valuable behavior, but not others.

- A single mentor who is too attached to the status quo can actually inhibit a protégé's development. A broader selection of mentors is likely to include people with new ideas that challenge the status quo.

- A single mentor may have a vested interest in keeping a promising protégé in his department or in the company, even when the protégé's highest potential lies elsewhere. Likewise, the single mentor may isolate the protégé from important outside information and discourage a career change that would be in the protégé's best interest.[4]

- A single mentoring relationship will not sustain an expanding career. Individual mentoring relationships are short-lived, seldom lasting more than a few years. The protégé must eventually say adieu to one trusted advisor and seek out another. A network of mentors provides continual support and learning.

- A mentoring network helps an individual to create productive alliances in different units of an organization and at different levels. Over time, those alliances can provide a huge career benefit.

Tips for Developing a Mentoring Network

- Make a list of learning needs within your own function and in others. Then approach people who can help.

- Get to know successful people in different functional areas of your company. One way to do this is to volunteer for cross-functional project teams. Your participation on those teams will bring you into contact with competent people from whom you can learn.

- Demonstrate your willingness and ability to return a favor. Mentoring is a two-way street.

Summing Up

- For new managers, a network of peers can be the key to a successful mentoring experience.

- One of the benefits of peer mentoring is that there are many more peers than suitable senior mentors available.

- Peers can provide many of the functions associated with traditional mentoring, but not all. Mentoring peers cannot provide the sponsorship, protection, challenge (through new assignments), and role modeling that many people need.

- Peer mentoring works best when these three conditions are present: (1) peers agree that each has something to learn from the other, (2) confidentiality can be maintained, and (3) each is willing to reciprocate.

- As you seek out mentoring peers, look for individuals who have an important workplace quality you lack, who are not intense competitors for the positions you seek, and whom you can trust.

- A "diversified portfolio" of mentors will provide a more complete spectrum of the career and psychosocial functions required by the upwardly mobile manager. So be prepared to develop a network of mentors.

The Eight Steps of Performance Appraisal

There is no one "right way" to conduct performance appraisal. Every company has a set of suggested procedures, and every subordinate presents a different challenge to the appraising manager. Still, effective practice generally involves the following eight steps, addressed in this order.

STEP 1: BE PREPARED Like every activity, performance appraisal benefits from preparation—by both employee and managers. Little can be accomplished if either manager or employee—or both—strolls into an appraisal meeting without having reflected on what has happened during the preceding months.

Let's consider the employee first. It is important to involve an employee in every stage of the appraisal process so that both sides of the story are on the table. One of the best ways of doing this is to have the employee complete a self-appraisal. In many cases, the human resource department provides a checklist for this purpose. That checklist states the employee's goals and the job behaviors and functions associated with them. (Note: Those goals should have been established with the employee at the very beginning of the appraisal period.)

In self-appraisal, the employee evaluates his or her performance against goals. If your human resource department doesn't provide a checklist, here are a few questions you should ask the employee to address in a self-appraisal:

- To what extent did you achieve your goals?

- Which, if any, goals have you exceeded?

- Are there particular goals with which you are currently struggling?

- What is inhibiting your progress toward these goals: lack of training, resources, direction from management, other matters?

Self-appraisal has two key benefits. First, it gets the person being evaluated involved. That involvement sets a tone of partnership for the appraisal process and makes the employee more open to subsequent feedback by the manager. Second, it gives the manager a different perspective on the subordinate's work and any related problems.

STEP 2: CONDUCT THE PERFORMANCE APPRAISAL MEETING
Many people are anxious about performance appraisal meetings. So create a tone of partnership from the very beginning. Start by setting the person at ease; don't let him feel that he is in the prisoner's dock. Then review the purpose of the appraisal and its positive benefits for both parties. This will psychologically prepare you and the employee and will act as a "warm-up" for dialogue.

Then ask the employee to talk about his self-appraisal. This will help you understand the employee's point of view and prevent you from controlling too much of the conversation. Listen very carefully to what the person is saying. Don't interrupt until the person has had his say. Demonstrate that you are listening by repeating what you've heard: "If I am understanding you correctly, you feel that you are meeting all goals with respect to the weekly sales reports, but that you're struggling to contact all the key customers you've been assigned. Do I have that right?"

Once the employee has laid all of his cards on the table, move on to your appraisal.

STEP 3: IDENTIFY PERFORMANCE GAPS As you disclose your appraisal, give priority to how the employee's accomplishments compare to agreed-upon goals. For example, if Joan says that her

greatest achievement was organizing and chairing a meeting between key customers and your R&D personnel, ask yourself, "Was
this one of her goals?" If it was, how close did that performance
come to meeting the metrics of that goal? How did she do relative
to her other goals? Look for gaps between actual and expected performance. Your big problem here may be that some performance is
difficult to quantify. For example, if a hotel manager has given his
desk personnel the goal of creating a welcoming environment for
guests, how would he measure their performance?

If your appraisal has found a "gap" between the employee's goal
and actual performance, make this the focus of your discussion and
feedback. As a starting point, identify a larger organizational goal to
explain how the employee's goal supports it. People can and do
change when they understand the consequences of their behavior
and work. For example, you might say:

> Our department's goal is to resolve all customer warranty problems
> within one week. That's our contribution to the company's higher goal
> of creating customer satisfaction and loyalty—both of which guarantee
> our future employment and bonuses. We can't accomplish that if any
> team member fails to handle his or her share of customer complaints.
> Do you see how what we are doing fits in?

Make sure the employee affirms your statement. Then move the
conversation toward identifying the root cause of substandard performance. "If you're falling short of your goal, why do you think that
is?" Listen carefully to the response; give your employee the first opportunity to identify the root cause. If you don't hear a thoughtful
reply, probe with other questions: "Could the problem be that you
need more training? Are there too many distractions in the office?"

STEP 4: FIND THE ROOT CAUSES OF PERFORMANCE GAPS
Identifying the root causes of performance gaps will, in most cases,
create an atmosphere of objectivity in which both you and your subordinate can contribute in positive ways. You won't be attacking the
subordinate, and he won't be defending himself from your criticism.
Instead, you'll be working together to address "the problem," which

in most cases is *outside* the subordinate (e.g., lack of proper training, too few resources, the workplace environment, etc.) The following suggestions can help you offer more useful feedback:

- Encourage the employee to articulate points of disagreement.

- Avoid generalizations such as, "You just don't seem involved with your work," in favor of specific comments that relate to the job, such as, "I have noticed that you haven't offered any suggestions at our service improvement meetings. Why is that?"

- Be selective. You don't need to recite every shortcoming or failing. Stick to the issues that really matter.

- Give authentic praise as well as meaningful criticism.

- Orient feedback toward problem solving and action.

(Note: For a handy checklist for planning a feedback session, see Appendix B. You can download free copies of the same checklist and other tools used in the Harvard Business Essentials series from the series Web site: www.elearning.hbsp.org/businesstools.)

STEP 5: PLAN TO CLOSE PERFORMANCE GAPS Once you've identified performance gaps and discussed their root causes, make sure that the employee acknowledges them and recognizes their importance. Once that is done, begin a dialogue about their resolution.

Give the employee the first opportunity to develop a plan to close any gaps. Say something like, "What would you propose as a solution?" Putting the ball in the employee's court will make that person more responsible for the solution and, hopefully, more committed to it. As the employee describes his or her plan to close any gaps, challenge assumptions and offer ideas for strengthening that plan. If the employee cannot put a credible plan together, you'll have to take a more active approach. In either case, seek agreement and commitment from the employee to the plan. A good plan includes

- specific goals;

- a timeline;

- action steps;

- expected outcomes; and

- training or practice required, if applicable.

The development plan should become part of the employee's record.

If you cannot settle the matter of closing performance gaps during your appraisal meeting, establish a time and place for a follow-up meeting, and explain its purpose. "Over the next week I'd like you to think about the things we've discussed today. I'll do the same. We'll then meet again and develop a plan for getting the help you need to handle these problems."

Before concluding the meeting, conduct a brief review of what was said and what agreements were made.

STEP 6: REEXAMINE PERFORMANCE GOALS Since an entire year may have passed since their last performance appraisals, reexamine the goals toward which your subordinates are expected to work. This is especially important when the organization is in a state of change, or when a subordinate is on a rapid trajectory of workplace mastery.

Involve the employee in the goal-changing process to be sure that (1) she has the capacity to assume new goals, and (2) she understands the details and the importance of these goals.

In all cases be very clear about the new goals and how performance will be measured against them. Also, depending on the employee's skills, this is the time to create a development plan (coaching, training, etc.) for giving the employee the capability required to meet the new goals.

STEP 7: GET IT ON THE RECORD It's very important to document your meeting, its key points, and its outcomes. That means that you'll need to take rough notes during the meeting and complete them immediately afterward, when your memory is still fresh. Make a record of

- the date;

- key points and phrases used by the employee (not necessarily verbatim), including his or her self-appraisal;

- key points and phrases used by you;

- points of disagreement, if any;

- a summary of the development plan;

- agreed-upon next steps; and

- performance goals for the coming year.

Chances are that your company will require that copies of this record be provided to the employee, to the employee's human resource file, and to your files. In most cases, both the manager and the employee are asked to sign the performance appraisal report, and the employee has a legal right to append his or her own comments to the report.

STEP 8: FOLLOW UP You should plan on following up every appraisal meeting. The high performers and satisfactory performers will obviously need less follow-up. However, if you've given them new, more demanding goals, you'll want to monitor their progress and determine if they need added training, coaching, or support.

Tips for Effective Appraisal

- Make the employee feel that he or she is part of the process.

- Provide honest feedback to the employees.

- Cover the full spectrum of the employee's job responsibilities in terms of what was done right and what was done wrong.

- Make it balanced: neither a lovefest nor total criticism.

- Identify what should be done in terms of employee development.

Employees with performance gaps who have committed to development plans should be more carefully monitored. That monitoring could take the form of a follow-up meeting every few weeks or months. Here, your goal will be to check for progress against development plans. These meetings represent opportunities for coaching and encouragement from you.

Useful Implementation Tools

This appendix contains tools that can help you become a better coach and/or protégé. These forms are adapted from Harvard ManageMentor®, an online product of Harvard Business School Publishing.

1. The Self-Evaluation Checklist (figure B-1). This is a tool you can used to evaluate your own effectiveness as a coach.

2. Planning a Feedback Session Checklist (figure B-2). This is something you can use to prepare for a feedback session with subordinates.

Coach's Self-Evaluation Checklist

The questions below relate to the skills and qualities needed to be an effective coach. Use this tool to evaluate your own effectiveness as a coach.

Question	Yes	No
1. Do you show interest in career development, not just short-term performance?		
2. Do you provide both support and autonomy?		
3. Do you set high yet attainable goals?		
4. Do you serve as a role model?		
5. Do you communicate business strategies and expected behaviors as a basis for establishing objectives?		
6. Do you work with the individual you are coaching to generate alternative approaches or solutions which you can consider together?		
7. Before giving feedback, do you observe carefully, and without bias, the individual you are coaching?		
8. Do you separate observations from judgments or assumptions?		
9. Do you test your theories about a person's behavior before acting on them?		
10. Are you careful to avoid using your own performance as a yardstick to measure others?		
11. Do you focus your attention and avoid distractions when someone is talking to you?		
12. Do you paraphrase or use some other method to clarify what is being said in a discussion?		
13. Do you use relaxed body language and verbal cues to encourage a speaker during conversations?		
14. Do you use open-ended questions to promote sharing of ideas and information?		
15. Do you give specific feedback?		
16. Do you give timely feedback?		
17. Do you give feedback that focuses on behavior and its consequences (rather than on vague judgments)?		
18. Do you give positive as well as negative feedback?		
19. Do you try to reach agreement on desired goals and outcomes rather than simply dictate them?		
20. Do you try to prepare for coaching discussions in advance?		
21. Do you always follow up on a coaching discussion to make sure progress is proceeding as planned?		
TOTALS		

When you have these characteristics and use these strategies, people trust you and turn to you for both professional and personal support.
*If you answered "**yes**" to most of these questions, you are probably an effective coach.*
*If you answered "**no**" to some or many of these questions, you may want to consider how you can further develop your coaching skills.*

Source: Harvard ManageMentor® *Coaching.*

Planning a Feedback Session

Use this tool to organize before giving feedback to anyone.

Name the issue or behavior that needs to be corrected or reinforced.

What is the organizational and personal significance of this issue?

What is the purpose of the feedback?

What details do you have to describe the behavior accurately? (who, what, when)

What is the impact of the behavior?

What results do you want to produce?

Who is the best person to give the feedback and why?

What communication style will be the most effective and why?

Describe possible barriers to giving this feedback. What can you do to overcome them?

What behavior on the other person's part would be more constructive? Why?

Source: Harvard ManageMentor® Giving and Receiving Feedback.

Notes

Chapter 4

1. This section is adapted from Harvard ManageMentor® on Giving and Receiving Feedback, an online product of Harvard Business School Publishing.

2. This section is adapted from Harvard ManageMentor® on Coaching, an online product of Harvard Business School Publishing.

Chapter 5

1. J. Richard Hackman, *Leading Teams* (Boston: Harvard Business School Press, 2002), 205.

Chapter 6

1. See Steven Berglas, "The Very Real Dangers of Executive Coaching," *Harvard Business Review*, June 2002, 86–92.

2. Monci J. Williams, "Are You Ready for an Executive Coach," *Harvard Management Update*, October 1996, 10–11.

3. Marshall Goldsmith, "Coaching for Behavioral Change," in Marshall Goldsmith, Laurence Lyons, and Alyssa Freas, editors, *Coaching for Leadership* (San Francisco, CA: Jossey-Bass/Pfeiffer, 2000), 22–25.

4. Gardiner Morse, "Behave Yourself," *Harvard Business Review*, October 2002, 22–24.

5. Marshall Goldsmith, "Coaching for Behavioral Change," 25.

Chapter 7

1. Chip R. Bell, "Mentoring As Partnership," in Marshall Goldsmith, Laurence Lyons, and Alyssa Freas, editors, *Coaching for Leadership* (San Francisco, CA: Jossey-Bass/Pfeiffer, 2000), 133.

2. See Kathy E. Kram, *Mentoring At Work: Developmental Relationships in Organizational Life* (New York: University Press of America, 1988), 22–39.

3. Gerald R. Roche, "Much Ado About Mentors," *Harvard Business Review*, January–February 1979, 14–28.

Chapter 8

1. Linda A. Hill, *Becoming A Manager* (Boston: Harvard Business School Press, 1992), 218.

2. Gerald R. Roche, "Much Ado About Mentors," *Harvard Business Review*, January–February 1979, 14–28.

3. "A Conversation with Nancy Nazir, " *HR.com*, <http://www.hr. com/HRcom/index.cfm/2/7EF06CE5-D4F4-4B6A-BACC435F724376 66?ost=feature> (accessed 21 November 2003).

4. Ibid.

Chapter 9

1. Linda A. Hill, *Becoming A Manager* (Boston: Harvard Business School Press, 1992), 218.

2. See Timothy Butler and James Waldroop, "Job Sculpting: The Art of Retaining Your Best People," *Harvard Business Review*, September–October 1999, 144–152.

3. Chip R. Bell, "Mentoring As Partnership," in Marshall Goldsmith, Laurence Lyons, and Alyssa Freas, editors, *Coaching for Leadership* (San Francisco, CA: Jossey-Bass/Pfeiffer, 2000), 140.

4. Herminia Ibarra, "Making Partner: A Mentor's Guide to the Psychological Journey," *Harvard Business Review*, March–April 2000, 147–155.

5. Ibid., 150.

Chapter 10

1. Martha Lagace, "How to Be Your Own Mentor," *Working Knowledge*, Harvard Business School online newsletter, 4 September 2001.

2. Kathy E. Kram, *Mentoring At Work: Developmental Relationships in Organizational Life* (New York: University Press of America, 1988), 106.

3. Felice N. Schwartz, "Management Women and the New Facts of Life," *Harvard Business Review*, January–February 1989, 65.

4. David A. Thomas, "The Truth About Mentoring Minorities: Race Matters," *Harvard Business Review*, April 2001, 99–107.

5. David A. Thomas, "Race *Does* Matter in Mentoring," *Working Knowledge*, Harvard Business School online newsletter, May 20, 2001; May 29, 2001.

Chapter 11

1. For the developmental and psychosocial functions of mentoring, see Linda Hill and Nancy Kamprath, "Beyond the Myth of the Perfect Mentor,"

Class Note 9-491-096, Harvard Business School Publishing, June 10, 1998. Also see Kathy E. Kram, *Mentoring At Work: Developmental Relationships in Organizational Life* (New York: University Press of America, 1988).

2. Linda A. Hill, *Becoming A Manager* (Boston: Harvard Business School Press, 1992), 226.

3. Ibid.

4. See Herminia Ibarra, "How to Stay Stuck in the Wrong Career," *Harvard Business Review*, December 2002, 42.

Glossary

ACTION PLAN   with respect to coaching, a clear statement of goals, measures of success, a timetable, and a clear indication of how the coach and the coachee will work together.

CLOSED QUESTIONS   questions that lead to "yes" or "no" answers.

COACHING   an interactive process through which managers and supervisors aim to accomplish one of two things: (1) solve performance problems, or (2) develop employee capabilities. That process relies on collaboration and is based on three components: technical help, personal support, and individual challenge.

DIRECT COACHING   a coaching style that is most helpful when working with coachees who are inexperienced or whose performance requires improvement.

MENTOR   a person who helps someone else experience personal growth through learning.

MENTORING   the offering of advice, information, or guidance by a person with useful experience, skills, or expertise to promote another individual's personal and professional development.

OPEN-ENDED QUESTIONS   questions that invite participation and idea sharing.

PERFORMANCE APPRAISAL   a formal method for assessing how well people are doing with respect to their assigned goals. Its ultimate purpose is to communicate personal goals, to encourage good performance, to provide feedback, and to correct poor performance.

PERFORMANCE GAP   the difference between a subordinate's current performance and what is required by the job—or by the job you'd like the subordinate to take on.

SKILL DEFICIENCY a gap between a person's current capabilities and those needed to take on another job.

SUPPORTIVE COACHING a coaching style in which the coach acts as a facilitator or guide.

360-DEGREE FEEDBACK a personal assessment tool used to systematically collect information about a person's behavior and performance from everyone who interacts with that person: boss, peers, and direct reports. The goal is to determine what it is like working for or with the person, and to isolate strengths and weaknesses.

For Further Reading

Notes and Articles

Higgins, Jaime and Diana Smith. "Four Myths of Feedback," *Harvard Business Review*, June–July 1999. Feedback is an essential element of coaching. A good coach knows how to give it and receive it. Why do people try to avoid giving or receiving feedback? No matter which end of it you're on, it's not easy. The biggest obstacles to constructive feedback are some myths about feedback itself. Contrary to popular belief, defensiveness is okay; mistakes should not be covered up or punished. The whole point of feedback, according to these authors, is to continually improve performance, and getting past the myths can help this happen.

Kegan, Robert and Lisa Laskow Lahey, "The Real Reason People Won't Change," *Harvard Business Review*, November 2001. Some coaching aims to change people—at least their behavior on the job. And as they may discover, changing behavior is a tall order. This article explains why it is often so difficult.

Every manager is familiar with the employee who just won't change. Sometimes it's easy to see why—the employee fears a shift in power or the need to learn new skills. Other times, such resistance is far more puzzling. An employee has the skills and smarts to make a change with ease and is genuinely enthusiastic—yet, inexplicably, does nothing. What's going on? In this article, two organizational psychologists present a surprising conclusion. Resistance to change does not necessarily reflect opposition nor is it merely a result of inertia. Instead, even as they hold a sincere commitment to change, many people unwittingly apply productive energy toward a hidden competing commitment. The resulting internal conflict stalls the effort in what looks like resistance but is in fact a kind of personal immunity to change. An employee who's dragging his feet on a project, for example, may have an unrecognized competing commitment to avoid the even tougher assignment—one he fears he can't handle—that might follow if he delivers too successfully on the task at hand. Without an understanding of competing commitments, attempts to change employee behavior are virtually futile. The authors outline a process for helping employees uncover their competing commitments, identify and challenge the underlying assumptions driving these commitments, and begin to change their behavior so that, ultimately, they can accomplish their goals.

Peiperl, Maury A. "Getting 360-Degree Feedback Right," *Harvard Business Review*, January 2001. Executive coaches use 360-degree feedback as a diagnostic tool to both uncover the strengths and weaknesses of their clients and to help those clients develop more accurate self-awareness. But what's the best way to use this tool?

Over the past decade, 360-degree feedback has revolutionized performance management. But one of its components—peer appraisal—consistently stymies executives and can exacerbate bureaucracy, heighten political tensions, and consume lots of time. Under what circumstances does peer appraisal improve performance? Why does peer appraisal sometimes work well and sometimes fail? And how can executives make these programs less anxiety provoking for participants and more productive for organizations? Peiperl discusses four paradoxes inherent to peer appraisal: (1) In the Paradox of Roles, colleagues juggle being both peer and judge. (2) The Paradox of Group Performance navigates between assessing individual feedback and the reality that much of today's work is done by groups. (3) The Measurement Paradox arises because simple, straightforward rating systems would seem to generate the most useful appraisals—but they don't. (4) During evaluations, most people focus almost exclusively on reward outcomes and ignore the constructive feedback generated by peer appraisal. Ironically, it is precisely this overlooked feedback that helps improve performance—thus, the Paradox of Rewards. These paradoxes do not have neat solutions, but managers who understand them can better use peer appraisal to improve their organizations.

Thomas, David A. "The Truth About Mentoring Minorities: Race Matters," *Harvard Business Review*, April 2001. Many companies hire the best and brightest, but then watch many promising minority employees get mired in middle management and leave out of frustration. This author identifies two very different career trajectories for whites and minorities and explains how mentors of minorities must operate in order to retain and support the careers of these individuals.

Waldroop, James and Timothy Butler. "The Executive As Coach," *Harvard Business Review*, November 1996. How do you deal with the talented manager whose perfectionism paralyzes his direct reports? Or the high-performing expert who disdains teamwork under any circumstances? What about the sensitive manager who avoids confrontation of any kind? Do you ignore the behaviors? Get rid of the managers? James Waldroop and Timothy Butler suggest that you coach them. They have found that coaching—helping change the behaviors that threaten to derail a valued manager—is often the best way to help that manager succeed. Executives increasingly recognize that it is people management skills that are the key both to their personal success and to the success of their business. And being an effective coach is a crucial part of successful people management.

Books

Bell, Chip R. *Managers and Mentors*, 2nd Edition. San Francisco, CA: Berrett-Koehler, 2002. A very popular and practical book, and a quick read. Bell introduces an approach for creating a learning organization one person at a time. Includes many practical tools, such as a self-diagnostic test to determine your readiness as a mentor.

Gilley, Jerry W. and Nathaniel W. Boughton. *Stop Managing, Start Coaching! How Performance Coaching Can Enhance Commitment and Improve Productivity.* Chicago: Irwin Professional Publishing, 1996. This book on performance coaching describes how managers can balance the roles of trainer, mentor, and career coach to improve workplace productivity.

Goldsmith, Marshall, Laurence Lyons, and Alyssa Freas, editors. *Coaching for Leadership.* San Francisco, CA. Jossey-Bass/Pfeiffer, 2000. This is a collection of original essays on executive coaching and mentoring contributed by prominent academics and practitioners. The material is of particular value to human resource professionals, trainers, and executive coaches.

Kilberg, Richard R. *Executive Coaching: Developing Managerial Wisdom in a World of Chaos.* Washington, DC: APA, 2000. The author provides a holistic view of coaching, showing how systems can be integrated into real-world coaching problems. In the complex and unpredictable world of business, Kilburg offers a practical and tangible guide for coaches to learn more about how to have a meaningful impact on behavior. He uses case studies, tables, and models for easy comprehension of a complex topic.

Kram, Kathy E. *Mentoring At Work: Developmental Relationships in Organizational Life.* New York: University Press of America, 1988. Harvard Business School professor Linda Hill has described this volume as "the most comprehensive and in-depth analysis of developmental relationships currently available."

Wellington, Sheila and Betty Spence. *Be Your Own Mentor: Strategies from Top Women on the Secrets of Success*. New York: Random House, 2001. Written by the president of Catalyst, a research organization that studies women in the workplace, this book underscores the importance of mentors for women who want to break through the "glass ceiling." It also advocates that women develop an executive presence, gain organizational visibility, and create a powerful network. The book is based on interviews with successful women in a number of industries, including Hewlett-Packard's Carly Fiorini, Avon's Andrea Jung, and lawyer Zoe Baird.

Zachary, Lois, J. *The Mentor's Guide*. San Francisco, CA: Jossey-Bass, 2000. This coffee table–sized book examines the process of mentoring from beginning to end: from assessing one's readiness to becoming a mentor to the natural conclusion of the mentoring relationship.

Index

About the Subject Adviser

HERMINIA IBARRA is the INSEAD Chaired Professor of Organisational Behaviour and Area Coordinator for the Organisational Behaviour Group. She received her M.A. and Ph.D. from Yale University, where she was a National Science Fellow. Prior to joining INSEAD, she served on the Harvard Business School faculty for thirteen years.

Professor Ibarra is an expert on professional development. Her new book, *Working Identity: Unconventional Strategies for Reinventing Your Career* (Harvard Business School Press, 2003), identifies the conditions that enable people to make major career changes. Her numerous articles on innovation, networking, career development, and professional identity have been published in leading journals, including the *Harvard Business Review, Administrative Science Quarterly, Academy of Management Review, Academy of Management Journal,* and *Social Psychology Quarterly*. Her studies and ideas have been profiled in a wide range of media reaching the general public, including the *Economist,* the *Financial Times,* the *New York Times,* the *Wall Street Journal,* and *Fast Company*.

About the Writer

RICHARD LUECKE is the writer of this and other books in the Harvard Business Essentials series. Based in Salem, Massachusetts, Mr. Luecke has authored or developed over thirty books and dozens of articles on a wide range of business subjects. He has an M.B.A. from the University of St. Thomas.